HONITON LACE
PATTERNS

Elsie Luxton

HONITON LACE PATTERNS

B T Batsford Ltd · London

ISBN 0 7134 4135 6 (cased)

Filmset by Latimer Trend & Company Ltd, Plymouth
and printed in Great Britain by
The Anchor Press Ltd
Tiptree, Essex
for the publishers
B. T. Batsford Ltd.
4 Fitzhardinge Street
London W1H 0AH

FRONTISPIECE

The Royal Christening Robe *(reproduced by
gracious permission of Her Majesty the Queen)*.

Made of fine Honiton lace lined with white satin
for Queen Victoria and worn at the christening of
the infant Prince of Wales, later King Edward VII.
In 1894 the robe was given by the Queen to the
Duchess of York, later H.M. Queen Mary, all of
whose children were christened in it. It was also
worn by the children of H.M. King George VI, the
Duke of Gloucester and the Duke of Kent, and by
the children of Her Majesty The Queen and H.R.H.
the Princess Margaret. It was last worn by Prince
William in 1982.

Contents

Introduction

My first book, *The Technique of Honiton Lace*, published in 1979 has found a warm response not only in this country but in most parts of the English speaking and lace making world. It has sold well in Holland, Germany and Belgium, traditional lace making centres where the techniques, because of our common origins, are closely allied to Honiton Lace and countries which I now visit regularly to give tuition. It has also recently been translated into Dutch. Lace makers in Australia, New Zealand, South Africa and Japan have also become keenly interested in this type of lace. Indeed, I was fascinated to find in my multi-national postbag a letter from a lace maker in Auckland, New Zealand, whose father was born a Tedbury, which was also my mother's maiden name; so as well as making new friends I have found a relative!

The purpose of writing this second book is to broaden the scope, not only of those who have mastered the most advanced Honiton techniques, but also of those who prefer to keep to the simpler patterns. Indeed, among the patterns in this book, some new, some traditional, there are plenty to occupy those who do not have a vast experience of Honiton lacemaking. Although raw beginners are advised to refer to the introductory chapters in my first book, instructions for fillings, leaves and general techniques have been included again for the convenience of ready reference by the worker.

Honiton Lace is worked with the right side of the lace underneath, so that the threads, when sewn and cut off, will be on the top or wrong side of the work. All the photographs in this book show the right side of the lace and are therefore a reverse of the prickings given. With the exception of three patterns all the samples shown have been worked with No.180 thread (Wrigleys). For patterns 1 and 2 I used No.120 Copley and Marshall thread; I also decided to use No.120 for my design for the Exeter Mayor's jabots in order to give body and strength to withstand laundering.

As requested by many students, I have included the numbers of pairs used for some of the patterns, but I must emphasize that consideration must be given to the thread used and the techniques gives a personal interpretation to the spacing of the pinholes of the patterns. Students' individual work and taste vary quite considerably, some preferring a close weave, others an open weave. The use of the various fillings and techniques gives a personal interpretation to the lace.

I wish to express my grateful thanks to my students past and present who have given me valuable assistance: Cynthia Voysey who has done the art work for my patterns and diagrams; Ruth Bickham who helped to check the script; Ronald Fisher who kindly typed the script and Elizabeth Prickett who contributed Method 3 for mounting the lace. My patterns 62 and 63 were worked by Elsie Johnson. Patricia Bury worked Pattern 60. The Wedding Veil was made by Shirley Martin. Among the patterns included are 54 of my own designs. Photography by Richard Tarr of Exmouth.

1
Beginners' Pieces

Pattern 1   Traditional shell

Use size No.120 thread, No.50 coarse thread. (Refer to photograph 1, pricking 2, and diagram 3.) Set up at A with six pairs and a coarse pair. Work in whole stitch to B and add one pair at this pinhole. Tie the runners after working through the coarse pair after this pinhole. Continue in whole stitch around the centre braid, working back stitches as needed.

When the braid reaches the first pinhole, A, sew one pair of runners and also the edge pair into this hole *(note 20f)*. Work the runners back to the other edge and make up the pinhole. Take out a pair of downrights. Work to pinhole B and sew the runners here after working through the edge pair on the outside, so that they will be in

position to use again as an edge pair after this second sewing.

After sewing at B, continue in whole stitch to start the outer section, adding pairs on the outside of the curve to make 11 pairs. Work the first section in whole stitch. Take the coarse thread through *(note 15)*. Work the next section in half stitch adding one more pair to make 12 pairs.

These 12 pairs will be sufficient to work around the alternate whole and half stitch sections, but reduce to 11 pairs for the last whole stitch section. Take out one pair from each side *(note 3a)*. Lay aside the coarse threads to be cut off later, after the sewing out has been made. Sew out two pairs into each of the four holes in the edge of the braid. Form into two bunches and cut off.

Fillings
The centre filling is Diamond *(filling 1)*. Leadwork Bars are worked in the other spaces *(filling 29)*.

1

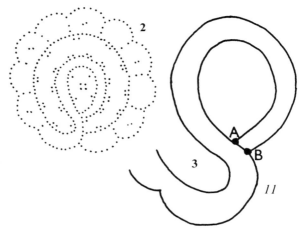

2

3

Pattern 2 Shepherd's crook
(simplified)

(Refer to photograph 4, pricking 5 and diagram 6.) Set up six pairs and a coarse pair at A, and add one pair at each of pinholes B, C and D. Tie the runners once after working through the coarse pair at each of these pinholes.

Continue working the braid in whole stitch with these ten pairs, making back stitches where necessary, and at the first curve.

When hole F has been worked, sew the outside runners across to hole E. Tie three times and put aside to cut off later. Continue with the runners and sew at holes D, C, B and A until the pinholes start again.

Sew a new pair into pinhole A for the new edge pair and third runners. Take out one pair on the inside at the start of the second curve and make back stitches as necessary. Continue round the third curve where the outside edge begins; purls may be made on this outer edge (note 9).

Work outer sections in half stitch, crossing the coarse thread between the sections (note 15).

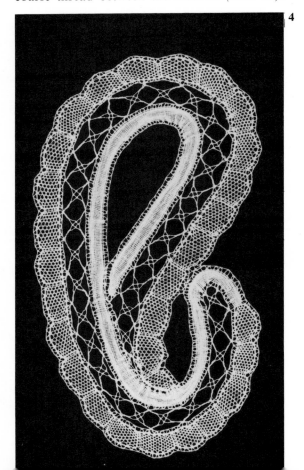

Upon reaching the completed whole stitch braid sew the edge pair into adjacent holes (note 20e).

Reduce to six pairs for the last section and sew out all pairs (note 23a).

Filling
Four Pin with Half Stitch Bars (filling 25).

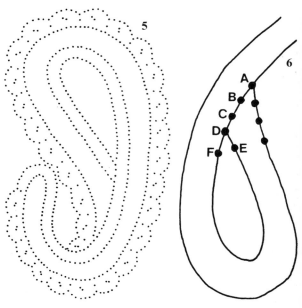

Pattern 3 Shepherd's crook
(traditional pattern)

(Refer to photograph 7 and pricking 8.)

Crook
Set up with six pairs and a coarse pair. This Shepherd's Crook is started in a similar manner to Pattern 2, but the pairs are increased to 16 for the whole stitch braid. Back stitches will be necessary.

Add one extra pair on the outside of the first curve and take out one pair at each of two holes on the inside just before the point of the curve and add them to the outside.

The two inside pinholes at the actual turn will need to be used three times each by working one back stitch; on the next return work to one pair before the coarse pair, leave the runners, use the last pair of downrights they worked through as new runners, work back to the outer edge.

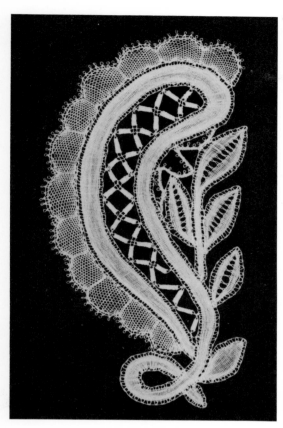

7

inside to the outside in whole stitch. At the first pinhole add one pair into the work and add one pair to lay back over the pillow to use later *(note 2d)*. Bring one coarse thread into position fifth from the outside; the other coarse thread will lie next to the sewings on the inside.

Work through the coarse pair and tie the runners once. Work one more pair, leave the runners and take the last pair worked as new runners back to the edge. Set the pin and add two new pairs as at the first hole. Repeat at the third and fourth pinhole.

Bring the pairs laid back into position to fill the gaps where the turns have been made at each hole. Work across in half stitch sewing the runners into the whole stitch braid. Continue in half stitch with 14 pairs, making purls on the outer edge and sewings on the inside.

To improve the shape and texture of the sections, take out one pair on each section one hole before the coarse thread is taken through *(note 15)*, and add one pair at the first hole of the next section each time.

Leaves
The four leaves are worked as Leaf 7, and the bottom leaf can be worked in whole stitch using six pairs and a coarse pair, increasing to 16 pairs then reducing to eight pairs for the stem. Sew out.

Fillings
Diamond *(filling 1)*; Purl Pin Bars *(filling 18)*.

Return to the inside and make up the back stitch. Two ordinary back stitches should complete the turn. Take out one pair at each of the next three holes on the outside of the curve, as this will now become the inside of the curve, where back stitches will be needed (13 pairs).

Take out two pairs and then sew out where the braids meet, as in Pattern 2. Sew in a new pair to use as outside edge pair and third runners. Work around the circle using 11 pairs. Back stitch on the inside and sew out into the braid. The small point should be worked by starting at the point with six pairs and a coarse pair. Sew out into the braid.

Half stitch edge
Sew five pairs into the two holes of the whole stitch braid opposite the first pinhole where the half stitch sections begin at the top. Weave the coarse pair through the centre three pairs of downrights and lay to the back. Work from the

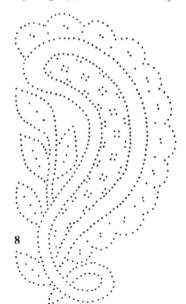

8

Pattern 4   Small daisy spray

(Refer to photograph 9 and pricking 10.) Set up seven pairs at the bottom of the main stem and work towards the flower, adding the coarse pair when the pinholes of the flower are reached *(note 22)*. A back stitch will be needed at the first pinhole on the outside. Work in half stitch adding extra pairs at both sides to make 12 pairs. Cross the coarse thread *(note 15)* between the petals. Back stitches will be needed on the inside of each petal. Reduce to eight pairs towards the end of the last petal and sew out into the pinholes of the first petal *(note 23a)*.

Start with six pairs and a coarse pair at the top of the bottom right-hand leaf *(note 1a)* and work in whole stitch. Increase to 12 pairs, reduce to seven pairs, sew the three pairs of runners into the main stem and carry these seven pairs forward to work the stem leading to the second daisy. Work this daisy as the first one. Work the three remaining leaves.

Set up at the top of the tendril above the flower with seven pairs and work in rib until the first half stitch section is reached. Add the coarse pair

(note 22). Working in half stitch, increasing to ten pairs. Cross the coarse thread *(note 15)* between the sections and work the central section in whole stitch with a Four Pin Bud *(note 11)*. The last section is worked in half stitch. Reduce to seven pairs and sew out *(note 23a)*. Repeat for the second tendril in a similar manner.

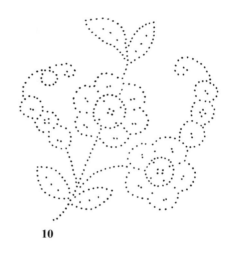

10

Pattern 5   Poppy

(Refer to photograph 11 and pricking 12.)

Stem and flower

Set up six pairs and a coarse pair at the bottom of the stem *(note 1a)* and add one pair at the second hole. Work in whole stitch with these eight pairs around the sepal of the flower. Take out one pair on the inside at the pinhole before the point and add one pair at the outer edge one hole before the point.

Cross the braids at the centre of the sepal of the flower *(note 16)*. Eight pairs can be laid in *(note 21)* and put aside while the whole stitch braid is being worked at the pinholes where the half stitch section will start. Complete the whole stitch braid and sew out into the stem.

Bring the eight pairs into position to work the half stitch section. Add the coarse pair *(note 22)* and work from the inside to the outside as back stitches are needed on the inside. Weave the coarse thread *(note 15)* between the sections.

9

14

Sew out all the pairs into the whole stitch braid but do not bunch.

Leaf

Set up six pairs and one coarse pair. Increase to 17 pairs. Work in whole stitch with a central vein. Reduce the pairs and sew at the stem side for a few holes before sewing out.

Pattern 6   Daisy

(Refer to photograph 13 and pricking 14.)

Stem and flower

Begin this pattern at the base of the stem with seven pairs. Work the flower as the flower in Pattern 4, increasing to ten pairs instead of 12.

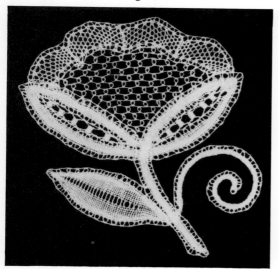

11

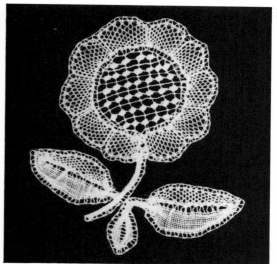

13

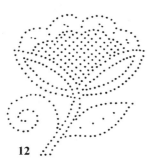

12

Leaves

Start at the small lower leaf with six pairs and a coarse pair and add one pair at each side to make nine pairs. Twist the runners twice to make a small vein. Reduce to seven pairs, take out the coarse pair. Rib along the short stem to reach the main stem, where the two runners are sewn and pairs are turned to work a rib up the stem of the large leaf. Add the coarse pair (note 22), and work as Leaf 1. Sew out. Sew in six pairs to start the last leaf.

Filling

Swing and a Stitch (filling 14).

Ribbed tendril

Work the tendril with seven pairs. Sew out into the stem.

Fillings

Pin and Stitch (filling 12); small Swing Lead-works are worked between the whole stitch braids (filling 30).

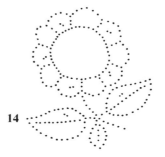

14

Pattern 7 Cross

(Refer to photograph 15 and pricking 16.) Set up on one of the top side points with six pairs and one coarse pair *(note 1a)*. Work in whole stitch towards the wide side of the curve. Do not add at the first hole, but add one pair at each subsequent pinhole on this side until there are 14 pairs.

Work down the straight in whole stitch. Work back stitches on the inner curve. Take pairs out until seven pairs remain when the third pinhole from the point is reached. Finish as in note 24.

Work the second central section (sewing it to the first length of braid). Work until the first mutual pinhole is reached and sew out the nearest edge pair, tie three times and lay aside to cut off later. The coarse thread will now lie next to the edge of the first completed braid; the runners are sewn at this side (without twists before or after the sewings) into each hole at the edge of the first braid. When these sections separate at the bottom a new edge pair will need to be sewn in. Complete this section as the first one *(note 24)*.

Work the two short side sections in the same manner, using 13 pairs. Sew out all pairs at each side into the centre braid. Do not bunch the threads.

For the half stitch points set up six pairs and one coarse pair *(note 1a)*. Add one pair on each side until there are 14 pairs in all. On reaching the whole stitch section sew out one pair of runners and the edge pair. Tie the edge pair three times and lay aside to cut off later. Work to the other side with the runners and repeat this sewing out at that side. Continue the half stitch, taking out one pair each side to reduce to six pairs before sewing out completely. Repeat for the other three half stitch points.

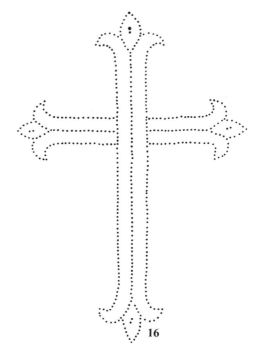

16

15

Pattern 8 Wild rose

(Refer to photograph 17 and pricking 18.)

Leaves

The lower spray of leaves is worked first. Set up at the base of the half stitch section of the centre leaf with six pairs and one coarse pair. Increase to ten pairs and reduce to eight pairs for the turn at the top. Work as for Leaf 1. Cut out the coarse

them again after the crossing has been made. Sew out all pairs but do not bunch the threads. A few pairs can be laid in and put aside to work the two small stems later. Work the top spray of leaves with a vein, using 13 pairs.

Filling
Diamond *(filling 1)*.

18

pair and work the short stem in rib with seven pairs. Carry the pairs forward, add a coarse pair and work the remaining two leaves. The main stem at the base can now be worked. Add one pair at each of the two holes before the point of the thorn. These two pairs are taken out immediately after. Back stitch on the opposite side. Sew out into the leaf.

Flowers
Set up on the outer first pinhole of a petal with six pairs and one coarse pair. Add one pair at each hole towards the centre pinholes of the flower, and also on several outside pinholes to make 15 pairs in all. Work in half stitch and take out one pair at each of the two holes before the crossing of the coarse thread between each petal. Add

2
Flat Patterns

Pattern 9   Damask rose

(Refer to photograph 19 and pricking 20.)

Flower and stem

Work the flower first. Starting at an outer point
of the whole stitch centre sections with six pairs
and one coarse pair, increase to 13 pairs then
reduce to work through into the second part.
Continue into the top outer half stitch petals

which will need 12 pairs. Work around the inner
petals taking sewings when the work reaches the
whole stitch sections. Sew out where the half
stitch began. A few of these pairs can be turned
and used to work the lower remaining petals. Sew
a few extra pairs into the outer pinholes ready to
start the first petal; then increase to 12 pairs,
complete and sew out.

Start at the bottom of the stem, working in
whole stitch up and into the sepal; here add one
pair at each of four holes on each side. Sew out
into the flower but do not bunch the threads.

19

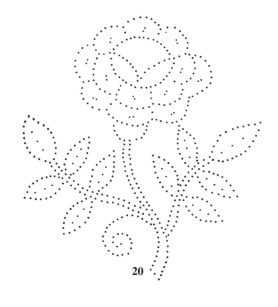

20

Leaves

The spray of leaves is worked from the top centre leaf. Set up six pairs, add one coarse pair and increase to 17 pairs. Sew out into the main stem. Each side leaf will start from the top point and sew out into the stem; these will need 13 pairs in all.

Pattern 10   Double horseshoe

(Refer to photograph 21 and pricking 22.)

First horseshoe

Work the toe clip of the complete horseshoe first. Set up at 1 *(diagram 207a)* with six pairs and a coarse pair and work as in note 34a. Continue in half stitch towards the point, taking out one pair at each side at each hole. At the point, lay the coarse pair back to cut off later, and tie the remainder of the threads into a bunch. Leave the ends long so that they may be drawn back when the sewings are taken here when working the whole stitch shoe.

At the top end of the same horseshoe set up six pairs and a coarse pair and work as in note 34a. Work the end of the horseshoe in half stitch and then cross the coarse thread *(note 15)* before working whole stitch. Increase to 19 pairs, adding these on the outside of the curve, working the nail holes as in note 13.

When the toe clip is reached, work across, taking sewings on the outside holes while back stitching on the inside. Complete the other side of the shoe to match the first part and finish as in note 34b *(diagram 207b)*.

Second horseshoe

Work the second horseshoe in a similar manner but sewing out into the first horseshoe. Work the second part of this horseshoe by starting at the top.

Ribbon

Centre knot. Set up six pairs and a coarse pair. Work first section turning into the second section as in Leaf 1. Work the loops and ends of ribbon in whole stitch or whole stitch and a vein, using nine pairs.

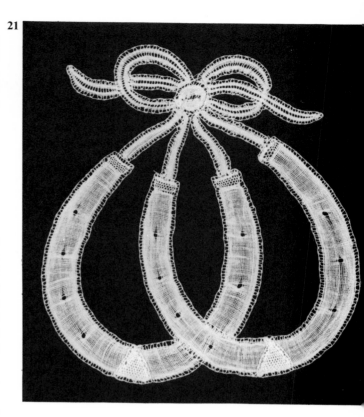

21

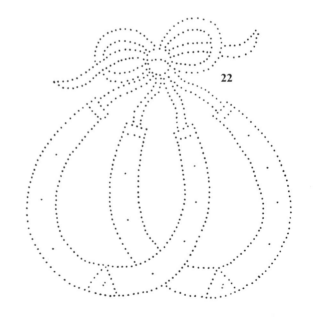

22

Pattern 11 Bell

(Refer to photograph 23 and pricking 24.) Set up six pairs and a coarse pair at the outer point of the bell *(note 1a)*, and work the inner braid in whole stitch. Add extra pairs *(note 2a)* on the outside of the curve to make 16 pairs. Reduce to seven pairs to work around the top narrow section of this whole stitch braid and increase to 16 pairs again as the pattern widens. Reduce to seven pairs for the turn into the half stitch section. Back stitches are needed on the inside of the curve. Tie well at the outer point and continue working in half stitch. Increase to 15 pairs gradually at every other hole on the outside of the curve. Reduce to ten pairs to work the top of this half stitch braid. As it widens increase to 15 pairs. Reduce to seven pairs before sewing out into three holes of the whole stitch braid at the starting point *(note 23)*.

Sew five pairs into the whole stitch braid for the Inner Vein Bar at the bottom of the bell. Weave the coarse pair through the downright

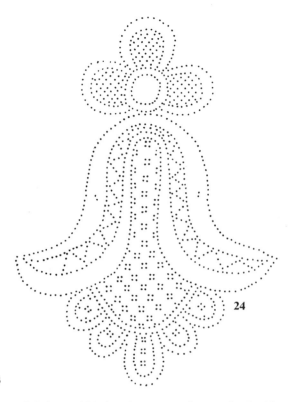

24

23

pairs *(note 22)*, leaving two pairs on the inside and one pair on the outside for the runners. Work to the outer edge of the braid and add one pair to make seven pairs in all. These seven pairs will be sufficient for this narrow bar. When the bar has been worked, sew the two pairs of runners into the opposite hole of the whole stitch braid. On the inner side tie the outer pair three times and put aside to cut off later. Use the other pair of runners to continue working and tie the runners after working the coarse pair. Work two more pairs, leave the runner pair and take the last pair worked through as new runners to work back again to the sewing side. Only one back stitch should be necessary on the inner side. When the sewing has been taken, work through all pairs and set a pin. Add two pairs to make eight pairs and when the outer pinholes start again, sew in one pair for the third pair of runners; this makes nine pairs in all.

Continue in whole stitch for all five sections at the bottom of the bell, turning into each section working as per note 30a.

The sections at the top of the bell are worked in **25** a similar manner, except that the inner circle is worked first. Set up at a pinhole where, when the circle is complete, the threads can be carried forward to work the other sections. Join by sewing at several holes of the circle where they meet at the top of the bell *(note 20e)*. Reduce the pairs for the turn so that only seven pairs are left after the turn to work the narrow part of the braid. Increase to ten pairs; the centre top braid will need 12 pairs.

Fillings

Diamond *(filling 1)*; Purl Pin Bars *(filling 18)*; Pin and Stitch *(filling 12)*; Four Pin with Half Stitch Bars *(filling 25)*; No Pin *(filling 4)*.

Pattern 12 Two bells

(Refer to photograph 25 and pricking 26.)

Ribbon and bells

Set up six pairs and a coarse pair to work the whole stitch ribbon loops first, and cross over the first braid to work into and around the first bell. Threads may be laid in *(note 21)* to use later to work the bars across the bell.

Sew out the whole stitch braid and now work the veined section of the ribbon. Work the second bell.

Clapper

Set up six pairs and a coarse pair to work the clapper and add one pair at each hole to make 11 pairs. Tie well back at several of the top holes. Reduce to six pairs and sew out.

Fillings

Italian *(filling 10)*; Purl Pin Bars *(filling 18)*.

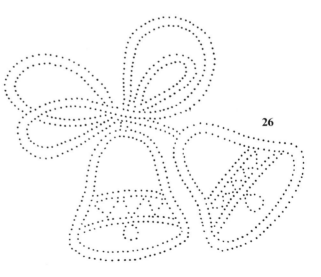

26

Pattern 13   Spray

(Refer to photograph 27 and pricking 28.)

Stem and buds

Set up *(note 1a)* at the base of the main stem with six pairs and a coarse pair. Add one pair at each of the first three holes on the outer side of the curve *(note 2a)*, and work in whole stitch with these ten pairs for the stem. Work up to the centre section of the top bud and, as this section widens, increase to 15 pairs. A vein has been worked up the centre of both buds in the example shown. Reduce to six pairs *(note 3a)* and finish off *(note 24)*. Leave the ends long so that when the top braid of the bud is worked, the sewing to join it can be more easily made by lifting this tied bunch. The ends are cut off close later.

To work one side of the bud, set up at one point with six pairs and a coarse pair. Work in whole stitch and increase by adding one pair at each side until there are 16 pairs in all. Reduce to six pairs, taking out more pairs at the sewing side. Sew out all pairs but do not bunch the threads. Repeat for the opposite side of the bud.

Sew eight pairs into the inner side of the whole stitch part of the bud at three holes where the top braid starts. Weave the coarse pair through the centre downrights *(note 15)* and work in whole stitch. Take out one pair as the narrow part is reached where sewings are made into the top three holes of the centre section. Add one pair to work the second half of this braid. Sew out.

The other bud will be worked in a similar manner except that the work will start at the point of the centre veined section, working into the stem with nine pairs and sewing out into the main stem.

Flower

Set up six pairs and a coarse pair for the inner circle of the flower and add one pair at the first centre hole and one pair at the first hole of the inner circle. Tie well back at these two holes. Start the inner whole stitch circle so that at the finish the threads are in position to work the five holes for the start of the half stitch petals. Complete the circle by sewing into three holes at the start of the braid. Some pairs can be brought forward and used to work the half stitch petals. Bring one coarse thread into the work for the outer edge; the other coarse thread will be cut off. Working as in note 34a, continue in half stitch and add pairs on the outer edge to make 16 pairs. Take out one pair at one hole before the petal narrows and add again immediately the petal widens. This process is repeated before and after the coarse thread is crossed between each petal. When the last petal is completed, a few pairs

27

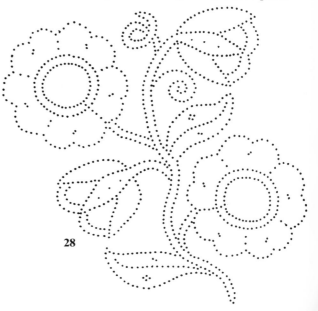

22

28

sewn out at the outer edge of the petal can be used for the short stem. Sew out into the main stem. Repeat as above for the second flower.

Leaves

Sew six pairs into three holes of the main stem where the whole stitch side of the leaf starts. Weave the coarse pair through the downrights. Increase to 14 pairs ready to work the four pin bud *(note 11)*. Reduce to seven pairs and work as Leaf 1, increasing to eight pairs to work the half stitch side.

Rib tendril

Work the Rib Tendril with seven pairs.

Solid tendril

Work the Solid Tendril with seven pairs and a coarse pair and cross the braid as in note 16.

Fillings

Swing and a Pin *(filling 11)*; No Pin *(filling 4)*.

Pattern 14 Sampler 1

(Refer to photograph 29, pricking 30 and diagram 31.) Commence at the outer pinhole of the half stitch centre section in a position where the finished threads will be carried forward to work the outside shapes. Set up with six pairs and a coarse pair and working in half stitch add extra pairs towards the centre holes of the section and increase to 12 pairs. Complete this half stitch section and sew out. Four of these pairs and the coarse pair can be brought forward to start the narrow whole stitch part of the first section of the outer border. The other pairs can be cut off. Increase on the outside of the curve to 15 pairs, but reduce to 13 pairs before the coarse thread is crossed *(note 15)* and use these 13 pairs for the half stitch section. The top centre section is worked in whole stitch, adding one more pair before working the four pin bud *(note 11)*. At the end of this section reduce again to 13 pairs for the half stitch section. The next whole stitch section will need 15 pairs and reduce to seven pairs to turn at the point into the second part of the sampler. Attach by sewing into the half stitch

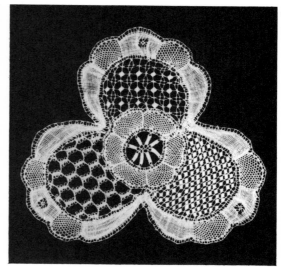

centre section as the turn is worked. Repeat the other two sections as the first and sew out.

Fillings

1. Devonshire Cutwork Variation *(filling 27)*. 2. Whole Stitch Block *(filling 22)*. 3. Four Pin and Leadwork *(filling 23)*. 4. Cartwheel *(filling 17)*.

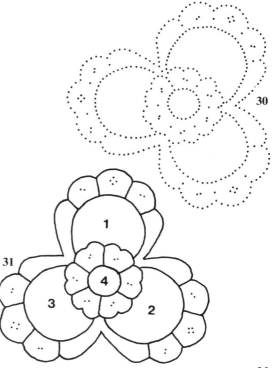

Pattern 15 Sampler 2

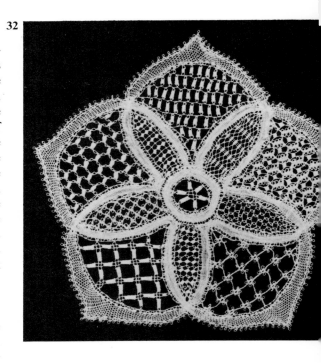

(Refer to photograph 32, pricking 33 and diagram 34.) Start with six pairs and a coarse pair as in note 1a at a pinhole on the outside of the centre circle in a position so that when the whole stitch circle has been completed and sewn out, the threads will be in position to work the outlines of the pattern. Increase to nine pairs for the whole stitch circle. These braids are turned at the centre as in note 30a and all the outlines can be continued. The threads will be sewn out when completed. These braids can be worked in whole stitch or half stitch, or as shown in the example with a half stitch outer edge which has purls *(note 9)*. Add one pair at each of the two holes before the point is reached and take them out after the point has been made.

Fillings

1. Straight Pin *(filling 21)*; 2. Toad in the Hole *(filling 9)*; 3. Blossom *(filling 8)*; 4. Diamond *(filling 1)*; 5. Brick *(filling 19)*; 6. Italian *(filling 10)*; 7. Pin and a Stitch *(filling 12)*; 8. Swing and a Pin *(filling 11)*; 9. Whole Stitch Variation *(filling 7)*; 10. Swing and a Stitch *(filling 14)*; 11. Cartwheel *(filling 17)*.

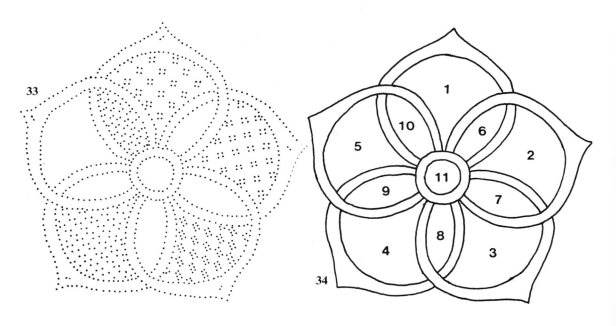

Pattern 16   Sampler 3

(Refer to photograph 35, pricking 36 and diagram 37.) Set up six pairs and a coarse pair at the point of the lower central braid. Increase to 11 pairs, one pair at each hole on the right. As the braid narrows, reduce to nine pairs and work around the lower shapes.

Turn as in note 30a and work the next section. Sew out.

To work the second central braid pairs will be sewn into the first central braid. The lower side section and the two top sections can now be worked before sewing out.

Leaves
The leaves are worked from the points and sewn out into the braids. The diagram shows: 3. Half Stitch Leaf; 4. and 7. Whole Stitch Leaf with Snatch Pin Hole; 12. Ladder Trail Leaf *(Leaf 7)*.

Fillings
1. Toad in the Hole with Wide Leadwork *(filling 24)*; 2. Devonshire Cutwork *(filling 26)*; 5. Blossom Variation *(filling 31)*; 6. Pin and a Chain *(filling 13)*; 8. Four Pin *(filling 6)*; 9. Cushion *(filling 32)*; 10. Four Pin and Leadwork *(filling 23)*; 11. Jubilee *(filling 3)*.

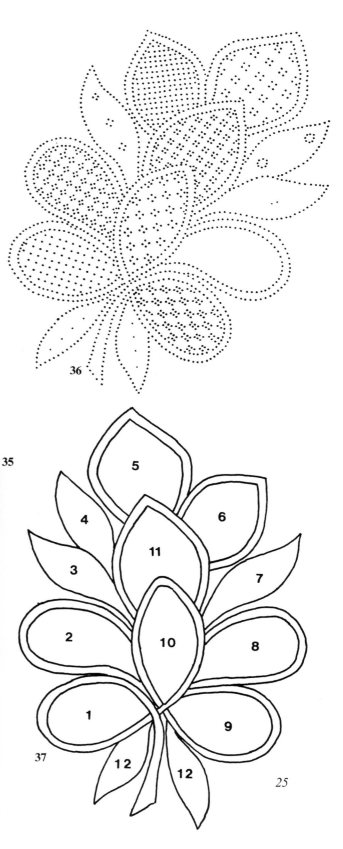

36

35

37

25

Pattern 17   Mat sampler

(Refer to photograph 38, pricking 39 and diagram 40.) This pattern is a traditional one and was originally used as an edging before being adapted and made into a mat. It enables the student to work up fillings which need quite a large space. It is advisable to use a large pillow as these fillings need many pairs of bobbins.

Start at the head of one of the outside scrolls and make a purl as in note 27. Work the braid in whole stitch increasing to ten pairs, taking out one pair on the inside at the turn of the scroll where three back stitches will be needed. Continue with nine pairs for the straight part of the braid, work into and complete the first of the three half stitch flowers. Work each scroll and first flower in a similar way. Work the remaining flowers in half stitch with purls *(note 9)* on the outside edge using nine pairs. Take out one pair at one hole before the coarse thread is taken across *(note 15)* between the petals, and add one pair again at the first hole immediately after the crossing.

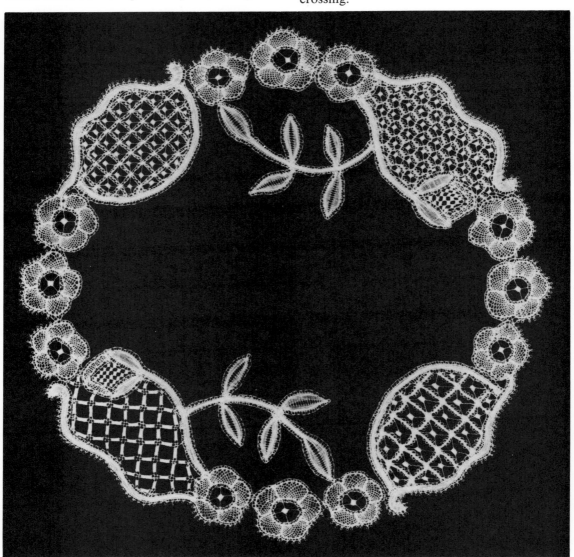

Work the inner braids in whole stitch and the top of the buds in half stitch.

Leaves
Start at the top pin of the centre leaf, attach to the rose before the leaf is started and sew out at the end of the stem. Work each veined leaf separately and sew out into the main stem.

Fillings
1. Toad in the Hole *(filling 9)*; 2. Rib Squares and Leadwork *(filling 20)*; 3. Diamond *(filling 1)*; 4. Snatch Bar with Leadworks *(filling 5)*; one Swing Leadwork *(filling 30)* is sufficient for the centre of the flowers.

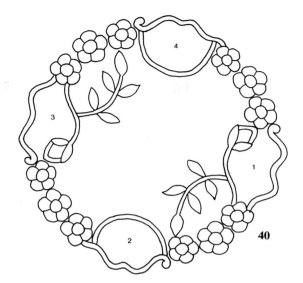

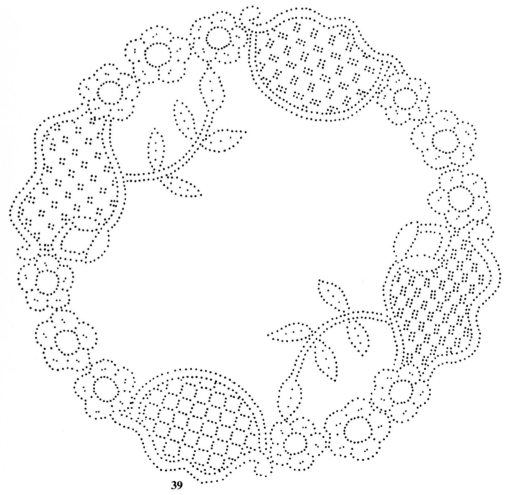

Pattern 18   Basket

(Refer to photograph 41 and pricking 42.)

Flowers
Work the centre flower first in half stitch with ten pairs but start in a position so that when completed and sewn out the threads can be carried forward to work the half flower.

Leaves and basket
These can be worked with a vein or whole stitch as desired. The whole stitch braid at the top of the basket can now be worked with ten pairs. Pairs may be laid in ready for the bottom of the basket as the top trail is being worked. The handle is worked in rib with seven pairs. When crossing the ribs, sew one pair of runners into a hole at each side; tie once and work two rows of rib without pins to enable the rib to reach the next row of pinholes. Here one runner should be sewn and tied once, ready to work the next section of rib. Sew out into the flower.

Fillings
Pin and a Stitch *(filling 12)*; Brick *(filling 19)*; Swing Leadworks *(filling 30)*.

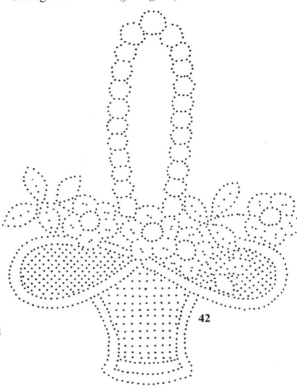

42

41

Pattern 19   Butterfly with Half stitch edge

(Refer to photograph 43 and pricking 44.)

Antennae, head, thorax and body
Set up six pairs to work each antenna in rib. Start in a position where when the top circle has been completed and joined, the threads will be in a position to work the curved line of pinholes. The pinholes should be on the outside of the curve.

Work both antennae towards the head and into the first hole in the top of the head. Hang two pairs on a pin in the centre pinhole and twist each pair twice. Twist one pair on the outside of both ribs three times each to become runners. Work one original pair of runners through to the outside to join one of these new pairs to make up the first pinhole. Work the other runners back

through two pairs of the other rib and leave to be a downright pair. The other original runner pairs will also become downrights. Weave a coarse pair through all downright pairs *(note 22)*.

Tie out one pair at one side, two at the other side, and cut off. Work in whole stitch and work the eyeholes *(note 13)*, having three pairs between the eyes. Take out one pair at each side before the coarse thread is woven through *(note 15)* at the start of the half stitch thorax. Take the coarse thread through again after working the thorax and then start the body. Work three rows of whole stitch before starting the ladder trail *(Leaf 7)*. Increase to 20 pairs and reduce to nine pairs before finishing off *(note 24)*.

Wings

Sew six pairs into the thorax to work the whole stitch trail of the top wing. Add the coarse pair *(note 22)*. Increase to 11 pairs towards the curve and one extra pair will be needed after the curve. Back stitches are necessary on the inside of this curve. Reduce to seven pairs and work as in note 30a for the turn into the lower wing whole stitch braid. Increase to ten pairs and reduce to six pairs

for the turn into the half stitch edge. Increase to nine pairs sewing on both sides for several holes. Sew in one pair for the edge runners where the pinholes start on the outside. Increase to 12 pairs for the wider part and use less pairs as the sections narrow. Weave the coarse pair between each section *(note 15)*. Sew out into the whole stitch sections. Work the opposite wings in a similar manner.

Fillings

Swing and a Pin *(filling 11)*; Pin and a Stitch *(filling 12)*.

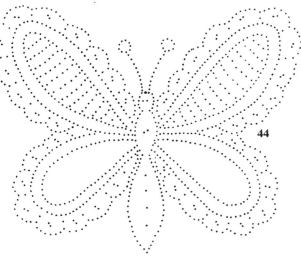

Pattern 20   Butterfly with relief wings

(Refer to photograph 45 and pricking 46.)

Antennae, head, thorax and body
Set up six pairs on each antenna, working in rib and having the pinholes on the top side. Work the head as instructed for Pattern 19, using ten pairs. Then take out one pair at each side before the coarse thread is woven across *(note 15)*. After the coarse thread has been woven across add one pair at each side and work in half stitch for the thorax. After completing the thorax take out a pair at each side. Take the coarse thread through again *(note 15)* and start the body. Work three rows in whole stitch and then start the ladder trail *(Leaf 7)* increasing to 16 pairs. Finish as in note 24.

Upper top wings
Set up eight pairs and a coarse pair in the top hole inside at the point of the inner row of pinholes to work the top relief wing. Work in half stitch and increase to 17 pairs. Reduce to seven pairs and lay back the coarse pair to cut off later. Sew the remainder into the head of the butterfly; tie into a bunch, but leave the ends long.

Lower top wing
Using the top hole of the second outer row of pinholes set up eight pairs and a coarse pair. Working in whole stitch, increase to 21 pairs. Work one centre and two side veins by twisting the runners three times as they pass through the downrights. Position the side veins two pairs from the centre vein. Reduce to ten pairs, sewing these out into the head and easing up the previous bunch to enable the sewings to be taken into the same holes. Use six pairs to turn into the bottom wing. Bring the coarse pair into position and work the whole stitch trail increasing to ten pairs for the wider part. Sew out into the side of the thorax.

Outer scallop rib
Sew in five pairs for the outer scallop rib. Work rib to the last hole of the first scallop. Add the pin, work through to the plain side of the rib and sew the runners into the wing. Tie once, put all pairs between this tied pair and tie twice. Roll this tied pair around the bunch to reach the first pinhole of the second scallop. Sew into an adjacent hole. Tie twice. Twist this pair three times and put it on the outside ready to use as the edge pair. Select an inside pair to use as runners to work out to the first pinhole of the second scallop. Continue making each scallop as above around the two wings. Sew out. Repeat these instructions for the wings on the opposite side.

Filling
Swing and a Pin *(filling 11)*.

Pattern 21   Daffodil mat

(Refer to photograph 47 and pricking 48.)

Flowers
Work the tip of the first stamen in whole stitch with six pairs. Change to a rib for the stem and turn at the base to work the second stamen. Tie

the threads in a bunch, leaving the ends long until the half stitch of the trumpet is worked. The bunch will then be drawn through and two sewings taken to attach the stamens as the half stitch is worked (15 pairs). Use a coarse pair for this half stitch, back stitching on one side towards the end so that the pairs can be carried forward to work one of the petals. Before this first petal can be finished, the pairs must be put aside until the whole stitch section of the trumpet has been made. To work the trumpet, sew 18 pairs into the half stitch section. Add a coarse pair *(note 22)*. Work to the end in whole stitch where the pairs will now be in position to work the centre petal, but before this is completed and sewn out, lay in pairs ready to work the next petal. When the third petal is complete, the first petal can be sewn out. Complete the flower. A second flower will have to be made and pinned onto the pattern before the corner leaves can be made.

Leaves

First work the leaf with a turned tip. Start at the point and work down one side of this leaf. Sew out into the flower. Work all leaves as shown in the example.

Fillings

Net *(filling 15)*; No Pin *(filling 4)*; Swing Leadworks *(filling 30)*; Pin and a Stitch *(filling 12)*; Swing and a Pin *(filling 11)*.

48

47

3

Edgings

Pattern 22   Edging for beginners

(Refer to photograph 49 and pricking 50.) This edging can be used on its own for a complete handkerchief edging or with any suitable handkerchief corner. It is a good exercise for basic stitches, purls and four pin buds.

Set up as in note 1a at the first pinhole on the straight side with six pairs and a coarse pair and work as in note 34a *(diagram 207a)*. Work the first section in whole stitch, increasing to 16 pairs. Cross the coarse thread *(note 15)* between the sections, taking out one pair one pinhole before this crossing and adding one pair again at the first pinhole of the following section. Work the second section in half stitch. Purls may be worked on the curved side as in the photograph, also the sections may be worked in whole stitch or half stitch as desired. Four pin buds may be worked in the whole stitch sections. Work the strip to the length required and finish as in note 34b *(diagram 207b)*.

Pattern 23   Leaf

(Refer to photograph 51 and pricking 52.) This very simple basic pattern is suitable for wedding veils or christening robes.

Set up six pairs and a coarse pair at the point of a leaf and work in whole stitch with a vein or ladder trail. Purl the outer edge and increase to 17 pairs. Reduce to eight pairs to work the stem, and having worked the second leaf, reduce to seven pairs at the point of the leaf and work into

the repeat of the pattern. Finish as in note 24. The half stitch sections on the outer edge will have purls and need nine pairs. The inner half stitch section will need one extra pair as there are no purls here.

Fillings
No Pin *(filling 4)*; Four Pin *(filling 6)*; Straight Pin *(filling 21)*.

Pattern 24   Simple scallop edging

(Refer to photograph 53 and pricking 54.) This is quite a simple edging suitable for a circular or square wedding veil.

Scallops
Set up with six pairs and one coarse pair *(note 1a)* in the top inner pinhole of the loop. Work the loop in whole stitch with eight pairs, making back stitches as necessary. Continue into the first scallop. Each scallop can be worked in whole stitch or half stitch or alternating whole and half stitch sections.

If purls are to be made *(note 9)* start these where indicated by the four small holes on the outside of the pattern.

When the next loop has been completed sew the runners on each side and work as note 16.

Flowers
Sew seven pairs into the scallop to work the stem in rib. Continue into the flower adding a coarse pair *(note 22)*. Work in half stitch and increase

to 13 pairs. Cross the coarse thread *(note 15)* between the petals and sew out as in note 23a.

Leaves

A vein may be worked in the leaves. Start at the point of the inner leaf *(note 1a)* and work across the stem sewing the runners into the rib. Work the second leaf and sew out the runners into the scallop *(note 23a)*.

Fillings

Put one single Swing Leadwork in the centre of the flowers and two Swing Leadworks in each loop *(filling 30)*.

Repeats of this pattern can be made. When joining the patterns it will be necessary to sew pairs into a loop, then work a section of scallop and join it to another already completed length.

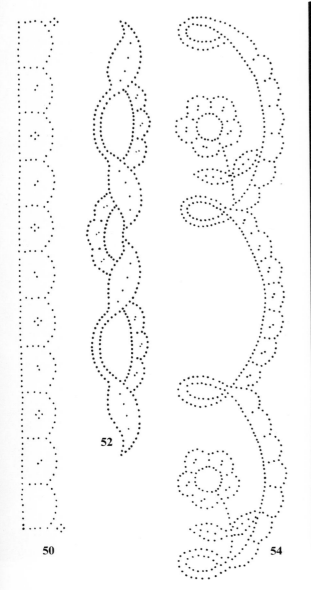

50   52   54

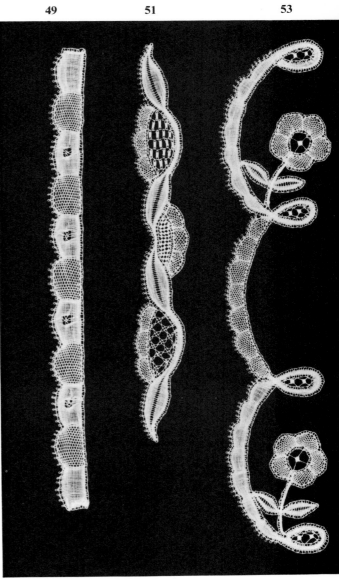

49   51   53

Pattern 25   Court edging

(Refer to photograph 55 and pricking 56.) Work the two flowers in half stitch first, setting up with six pairs and a coarse pair. Increase to 13 pairs and purl where indicated. Take one pair out at one hole before the crossing of the coarse thread and add one pair again immediately the next petal starts. Sew out all pairs. Sew pairs into the flower where the single whole stitch trail starts. (If this flower is worked last, a few pairs can be brought forward and used with the pairs sewn in.) Work to the division of the trail and proceed as in note 17. Complete one trail and sew out into the opposite flower – the inner trail will need 14 pairs, the outer trail which will have purls will need 12 pairs. Sew the pairs into the flower for the half stitch sections (13 pairs). Sew out into the trail. The ends will not show behind the whole stitch.

Fillings

Four Pin *(filling 6)*; Blossom *(filling 8)*; Cartwheel *(filling 17)*; Toad in the Hole with Wide Leadwork *(filling 24)*.

Pattern 26   Clyst edging

(Refer to photograph 57 and pricking 58.)

Flower

Set up seven pairs and a coarse pair at an outside pinhole where a petal starts. Work towards the centre circle of holes, make a back stitch and add two pairs at each of the next two holes. Tie well back after the coarse thread has been worked, and increase to 15 pairs for the half stitch flower. Take out one pair just before each petal narrows and also before the coarse thread is taken across. Add one pair again immediately the pattern widens and the next petal starts. Sew out all pairs at the finish.

Leaf

The whole and half stitch leaf is worked first. Sew eight pairs into the flower where the whole stitch side begins and increase to 14 pairs. Reduce to six pairs as the work passes into the turned tip which

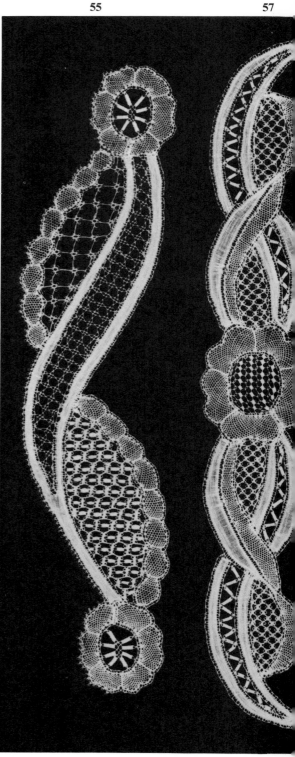

should be worked in half stitch with 12 pairs. Gradually reduce to six pairs at the tip, taking out the coarse pair and tie the other threads into a bunch, leaving the ends long until the next leaf is worked. Sewings are then taken into two holes at this point, and the ends cut off later. The whole stitch section of the first leaf will need 11 pairs at the widest point, but reduce before sewing out into the flower. (A few pairs can be laid in and put aside for this whole stitch section as the work proceeds into the tip.) The whole stitch braid leaf will need 12 pairs, reducing to six pairs to turn at the top. Add one pair one hole before the point and tie well back after the coarse pair has been worked.

The pairs for one of the lower whole stitch braids of the leaf are sewn into the half stitch side of the first leaf. Sew out into the flower. To complete this leaf a few pairs may be turned and used to work up the second section, and are then sewn out into the half stitch side of the leaf.

Fillings
Swing and a Pin *(filling 11)*; Whole Stitch Block Variation *(filling 7)*; Leadwork Bars *(filling 29)*.

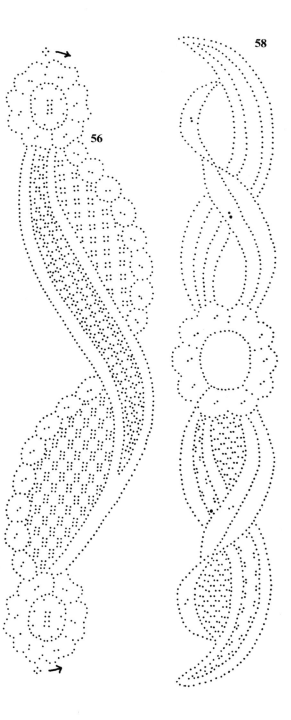

56

58

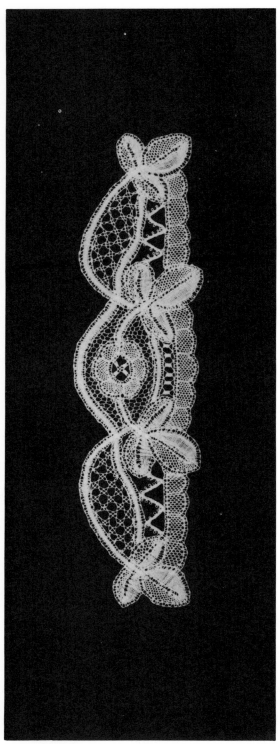

59

Pattern 27   Mayoral edging

(Refer to photographs 59 and 60 and pricking 61.) Start the flower petal in a position so that when completed the threads will be ready to use for one of the centre sprays of leaves. Work with six pairs and a coarse pair and increase to nine pairs. Turn and work the threads into the stem of the first spray of leaves using six pairs and a coarse pair.

Work into the half stitch section of the leaf and work as for Divided Leaf *(Leaf 1)*. Reduce to six pairs for the top of the leaf and increase to ten pairs for the whole stitch side.

Work the threads around and into the side leaf nearest to the flower using eight pairs for the whole stitch and six pairs for the half stitch.

61

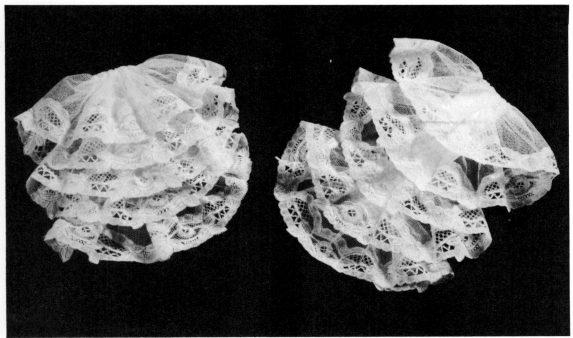

Cross to the third leaf and when complete, carry the pairs forward to make the stem and outer spray of leaves, then sew out. Sew pairs into the opposite side of the flower and complete the two leaf sprays on the other side.

Using six pairs and a coarse pair work the whole stitch trail from one outer spray of leaves across the stems to the other side, joining the stems where they cross. Work the half stitch sections between the leaves with 11 pairs. Sew out into the whole stitch side of the leaves where possible and do not bunch the threads. Purls may be added on the outside edge. Make a Whole Stitch Bar to connect the two central leaf sprays, or the space may be used for a filling.

Fillings

Purl Pin Bars *(filling 18)*; Four Pin *(filling 6)*; Trolley Net *(filling 15)*; Swing Leadworks *(filling 30)*; Diamond filling in flower *(filling 1)*.

The bottom section of half stitch scallops may be added or omitted depending on the width of edging desired. The example shown is suitable for a veil, but after I designed this pattern I added the extra half stitch section to get the required width for the jabots made for the Mayor of Exeter. This extra half stitch section is included in the pricking.

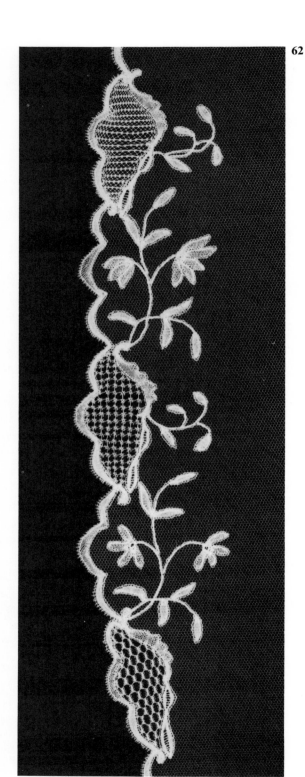

62

64

Flowers
These have a rib stem which continues into and around the centre of the flower; the pairs can then be carried forward to complete the petals, all worked as per instructions for Raised Leaf with Taps *(Leaf 6)*.

Leaves
All leaves have been worked with a rib stem and completed as for Simple Raised Leaf *(Leaf 4)*.

Fillings in the sample edging
Italian *(filling 10)*; Blossom *(filling 8)*; Whole Stitch Block *(filling 22)*.

Pattern 28   Exmouth edging

(Refer to photographs 62 and 63 and pricking 64.) This is a traditional Devon pattern found many years ago by a local butcher at Exmouth, and worked recently by one of my Exmouth students in making the wedding veil shown in the photograph. One complete section of this edging consists of three filling parts, with two different sprays of flowers between them. Therefore the two end sections which have fillings will need to be worked first, and these sections pinned back on the complete pattern to work the centre.

Filling sections
Begin the sections by working the inner half stitch braid, finishing as in note 24. The outer braid and the ladder trail braid can now be worked and sewn out into the first braid. Work the centre filling section as the other two, except that the longer outer braid with points can be started at the scroll end and sewn out into one of the completed sections. The shorter outer braid is worked separately and sewn out. A coarse pair should be used in all unraised braids.

4
Handkerchiefs

Pattern 29   Rose corner

(Refer to photograph 65 and pricking 66.)

Flowers
Set up six pairs and a coarse pair at the centre of
the rose for the whole stitch section *(note 1a)*.
Add one pair at the outside at each hole to make
16 pairs. It will be necessary to make back

stitches at almost every hole on the inner curve,
starting at the second hole. Reduce gradually to
eight pairs to work through to the start of the half
stitch petals. Work as in note 34a. Use 15 pairs,
and cross the coarse thread between sections
(note 15). Use 14 pairs when starting the purls
(note 9) for the outside edge.

Complete the flower and sew out each pair at

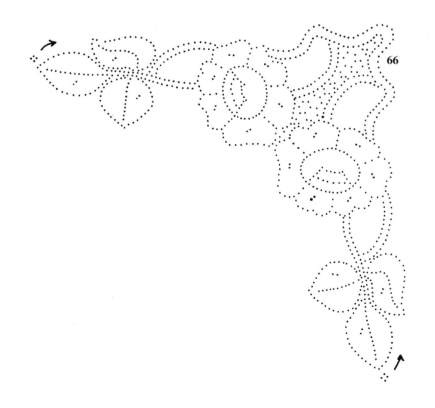

66

the start of the first petal. Do not bunch. Repeat these instructions for the other flower.

Outer corner braid

Sew six pairs into the edge of the flower at the start of the whole stitch trail. Add the coarse pair *(note 22)*. Work to the outside edge for the first hole. Several back stitches will be necessary to work the curves. Sew out all pairs into the opposite flower. Sew six pairs into the half stitch flower, add the coarse pair and work the Whole Stitch Bars. Sew out into the outer trail. Sew six pairs into the edge of the rose, add the coarse pair *(note 22)* and work as for Divided leaf *(Leaf 1)* for the three leaves. Work purls where indicated. Work the short whole stitch trail.

Fillings

Straight Pin *(filling 21)*; Whole Stitch Block Variation *(filling 7)*; Swing and a Pin *(filling 11)*.

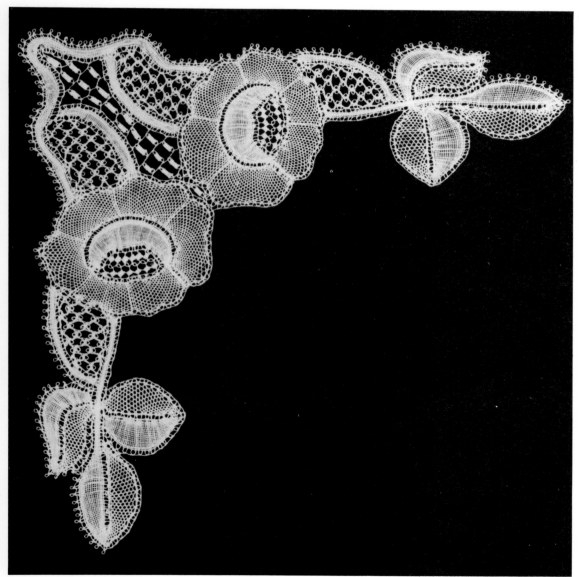

Pattern 30 Heart corner

(Refer to photograph 67 and pricking 68.)

Heart

Start at the scroll end of the heart in whole stitch with six pairs and a coarse pair *(note 1a)* and increase to 12 pairs. Tie back at each hole on the outside edge, and on the inside work back stitches as necessary, taking out two pairs as these back stitches are made. Work with ten pairs on the straight.

Before the purl edge starts, take out two pairs. Work around the point and add one pair at the hole before the point. Tie well back at this point and take one pair out on the inside where back stitches are needed. When the purl edge ends, add two pairs to make ten pairs again. Attach to the first scroll by sewing to the four holes where the pinholes meet *(note 20e)* and then increase to 12 pairs to work the scroll. Four pairs can be laid aside to use later for the inner trail and two pairs laid back at the other side to use as in note 24 for the finish.

For the inner whole stitch braid, sew in pairs to make seven pairs in all and add the coarse pair *(note 22)*. Add one pair to make nine pairs. Reduce to eight pairs as the braid narrows and add one pair again towards the finish and sew out into the scroll.

Outer side whole stitch scroll and leaves

Set up six pairs and one coarse pair *(note 1a)*. Add one pair at each hole at each side to make 14 pairs. Tie well back at each hole and work as note 31a. When the pinhole on the inside is reached where the actual turn is made, reduce to 12 pairs. Continue in whole stitch and remember to make purls *(note 9)* on the outer edge for about nine holes.

At the end of the scroll section turn into the whole stitch section of the outside leaf. With four pairs only work purls immediately on the outside edge. Sew on the other side until the pinholes are reached. Add pairs gradually until there are 13 pairs in all for the whole stitch outer side of this leaf. Reduce to seven pairs for the turn at the top of the leaf and work as for Divided leaf *(Leaf 1)*.

67

Purl on the last top hole before sewing to the hole of the scroll. Reduce to four pairs and sew out. Sew in pairs for the second leaf and work as for Leaf 1.

Small centre leaf and smaller side leaves

The centre leaf is worked as for Ladder Trail Leaf *(Leaf 7)* and the smaller side leaves are worked with a vein.

68

Fillings

Brick *(filling 19)*; Diamond and Leadwork Bars *(fillings 1 and 29)*; Pin and a Stitch *(filling 12)*.

Pattern 31   Half stitch corner

(Refer to photograph 69 and pricking 70.)

Whole stitch scroll

Set up with six pairs and a coarse pair *(note 1a)*. Start with a purl *(note 27)* for the whole stitch scroll. Work back stitches on the inside of the scroll and increase to ten pairs on the outside. Take out one pair on the inside of the scroll and work the braid with nine pairs. Just before the scroll at the opposite side, add one pair on the outside edge. Work back stitches on the inside of the scroll and lay aside pairs at each hole, also add two pairs and lay aside. These pairs will be used to start working the half stitch sections. Work purls as indicated on the pattern.

Half stitch sections

Bring the pairs laid aside into position ready to start the half stitch section. Add the coarse pair *(note 22)*. Ten pairs are needed for these half stitch sections. Work around the half stitch edge and sew out.

Centre leaves

The centre leaf is worked in ladder trail *(Leaf 7)*. 17 pairs are needed. The side leaves have veins and need 15 pairs.

Whole stitch trail

The whole stitch trail will need nine pairs. The inside half stitch edge will need 12 pairs. Take out one pair before the coarse thread is taken across *(note 15)* and add one pair at the start of the next section. Sew out.

Fillings

Straight Pin *(filling 21)*; Four Pin *(filling 6)*; Purl Pin Bars *(filling 18)*; Diamond *(filling 1)*.

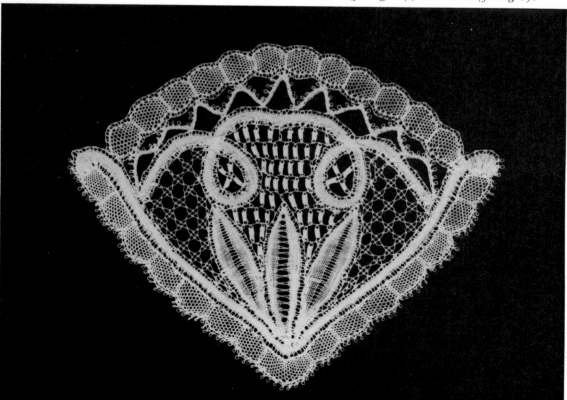

Pattern 32   Periwinkle

(Refer to photograph 71, pricking 72 and diagrams 73a and 73b.)

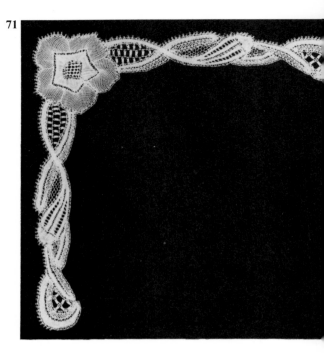

Flower

Set up six pairs and a coarse pair at A *(diagram 73a)*. If you first work in whole stitch to the outside hole B, where there are more holes at this side, fewer back stitches will be needed on the inside. Add one pair at holes C, D and E, tying back each time after the coarse pair has been worked. Add one pair on the outside at the third and second holes before the point. Tie after the point hole. Take out one pair after each point has been made, reducing to ten pairs between each point. Add the two extra pairs two holes before each point and reduce to nine pairs at the end of this last section before sewing out into pinholes A, C and E. The last section will need a back stitch at each hole. Bring five of these pairs, including the coarse pair, into position to work the outer half stitch section. Work as in note 34a *(diagram 207a)*. Work in half stitch to the sewing side; each hole will need two sewings. Add one pair at the hole before the point on the outside, taking out one pair at the inside at this point. Work purls *(note 9)* on the outside where indicated. One pair less will be needed where purls are made. Add this pair again when the purl edge ends. Work all sections and sew out.

First leaf

Start at A *(diagram 73b)* at the side of the leaf with six pairs and a coarse pair *(note 27)*. Work in whole stitch to B, add one pair and make a purl. Work to C. Back stitches will be needed at every hole on this side and pairs may be laid in and put aside in readiness to use later to work one side of the lower part of this leaf. Pairs will be sewn in later to work the second half.

At the outer edge one pair is added at each hole except the hole at the point. After the point of the leaf has been made, take out one pair on the outside edge at each hole, reducing to four pairs, including the coarse pair. These pairs will be used for one half of the ladder trail *(Leaf 7)*. Bring the pairs laid aside into position and add the coarse

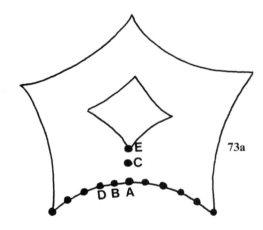

73a

pair *(note 22)*. Work one row of whole stitch and start the ladder trail. Start with three twists and at the finish reduce to two and then one twist. Fourteen pairs are used for the top, reducing to eight pairs as the ladder trail ends. Sew in the pairs to work the second ladder trail section, reducing to five pairs when the two sections meet. Work across all pairs of both sections, laying aside the middle coarse threads to be cut off later. Sew out into the flower.

Second leaf

Sew six pairs into the lower petal of the flower, add a coarse pair, then working in whole stitch add one pair to make eight pairs. Sew into the stem of the first leaf and cross the braids *(note 16)*. Add one pair and start the purl edge *(note 9)*. Reduce to five pairs at the top of the leaf and work as for Leaf 1. Sew into the first leaf where the pinholes meet, cross the stem once again and complete.

Third leaf

Sew in five pairs at the top of the first leaf to work the whole stitch section. Add a coarse pair. Use these six pairs to work as for Leaf 1.

Fourth leaf

Sew five pairs into the side of the first leaf for the whole stitch section. Both sections of the lower part of the leaf are worked first and sewn out, the top part of the leaf being worked later. The turning of this first part is worked according to note 30a.

For the top part of the fourth leaf, six pairs are sewn into the side of the third leaf. Add a coarse pair. Increase to 11 pairs, then reduce to six pairs to turn the top of this leaf. Use these six pairs to work the half stitch side. Sew out.

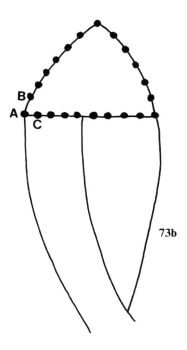

73b

Fillings

Diamond *(filling 1)*; Trolley Net *(filling 15)*; Straight Pin *(filling 21)*; No Pin *(filling 4)*.

Four of these corners make a complete handkerchief edging.

72

Pattern 33   Fan corner

(Refer to photograph 74 and pricking 75.) Start the whole stitch trail at a pinhole on the side of the second leaf *(note 1a)*. Add one pair at the next two holes on the leaf side. Increase to ten pairs. When purls start at the corner take out one pair and use nine pairs. Before this trail can be completed put aside the nine pairs, work the centre leaf in ladder trail *(Leaf 7)* with 16 pairs. Work the next leaf with a four pin bud *(note 11)* and use 15 pairs. The outer trail can now be completed and sewn out into this leaf. Work the other leaf with a four pin bud and the remaining two leaves with a vein.

Work the corner in half stitch using ten pairs and make purls *(note 9)* on the outside edge. Work the three stems in whole stitch; the centre stem will start with 12 pairs sewn into the half stitch edge.

Fillings
Brick *(filling 19)*; Toad in the Hole *(filling 9)*; Trolly Net *(filling 15)* between the stems.

Pattern 34   Leaf and trail corner

(Refer to photograph 76 and pricking 77.) Start as in note 1a on the inside of one of the side sections and work the whole stitch trail. Add one pair one hole before the points on the trail. Work purls where indicated *(note 9)*. Complete the trail and sew out opposite the start *(note 23a)*.

Work the centre trail with seven pairs in whole stitch with a vein. When pairs are sewn out after the second crossing of the whole stitch trail use the pairs to start working a leaf. Increase to 16 pairs for the half stitch side and remember to work purls *(note 9)* when the outer edge is reached.

Turn the top of the leaf with five pairs as Leaf 1. Increase to 13 pairs for the whole stitch side of the leaf. Sew out. To work the second leaf, start by sewing pairs into the veined braid and work the whole stitch side first. Complete as first leaf. Pairs are sewn into the leaf for the top corner. Use 12 pairs for the half stitch sections. Add two pairs for the whole stitch section and work a four pin bud *(note 11)*. The extra pairs will need to be taken out again for the half stitch sections. Sew out into the opposite leaf.

Fillings
Diamond *(filling 1)*; Purl Pin Bar *(filling 18)*; Brick Variation *(filling 28)*.

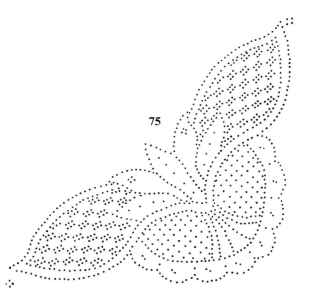

75

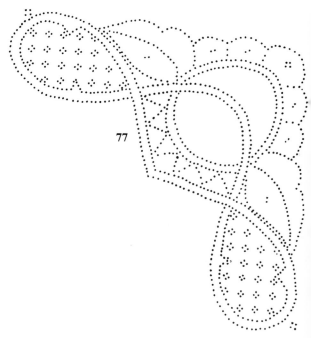

77

Pattern 35   Leaf corner

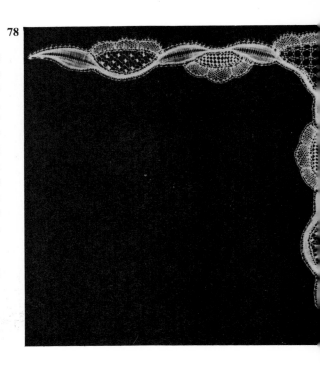

(Refer to photograph 78 and pricking 79.) This is a very basic pattern. Start at the side point of the first leaf with six pairs and a coarse pair. Purl the outer edge. A vein or ladder trail may be worked, increasing to 17 pairs. Reduce to eight pairs for the stem of the leaf and to six pairs for the narrow braid between the leaf tips. Continue working all leaves to the opposite side of the corner and finish as in note 24. The half stitch sections can now be worked. Sew in the pairs where each section starts and add a coarse pair *(note 22)*. Purl on the outer edge and sew out all pairs when complete.

Fillings
No Pin *(filling 4)*; Four Pin *(filling 6)*; Spotted Net *(filling 16)*.

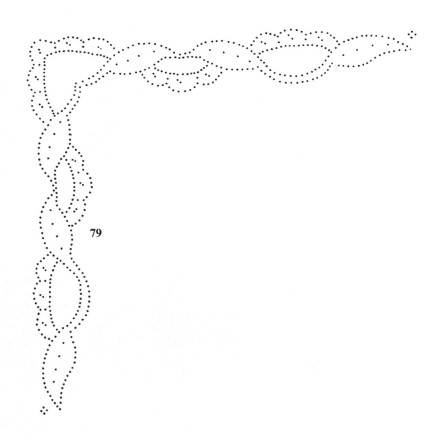

79

Pattern 36   Turkish corner

(Refer to photograph 80 and pricking 81.) Set up six pairs and a coarse pair where the braids meet at the sides. Work the outer braid for the side point; add two more pairs and work purls on the outer edge until the side point is reached. Take out one pair on the inside, where the last hole will need a back stitch, and add one pair at one hole before the point on the outside. To turn this point it will be necessary to work within three pairs of the back stitch, leave the runner pair and take the last pair worked through as new runners to work to the outside edge. Next, work to within two pairs of the back stitch and repeat until the back stitch is made up. A sewing will be needed on the inside of the next hole. Make up the edge stitch and sew the outer pair of runners into one hole before the inner back stitch hole. Take out the pin from the back stitch hole and gently pull the coarse thread here; this enables the braid to lie flat at this sharp turn of the pattern. Continue the whole stitch braid and work as in note 30a. Turn into the half stitch corner section using seven pairs; complete and sew out. Work the

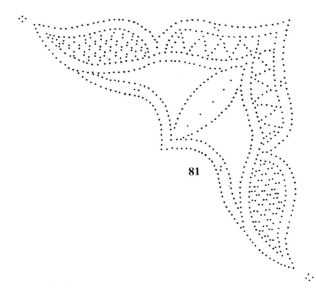

inner half stitch braid. The centre leaf has been worked as for the ladder trail leaf *(Leaf 7)*.

Fillings
Whole Stitch Block Variation *(filling 7)*; Devonshire Cutwork *(filling 26)*; Purl Bin Bars *(filling 18)*.

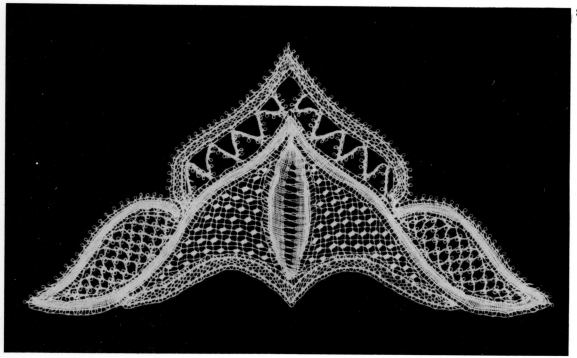

5

Small Motifs

Pattern 37a   Owl on Moon

(Refer to photograph 82, pricking 83 and diagram 84.)

Moon

Set up at the top pinhole of the moon as in note 1a. Work in whole stitch for five rows and then add pairs gradually *(note 2a)* on the outer side at every other hole to make 14 pairs. Reduce to ten pairs and make two holes *(note 13)* to represent the feet. Reduce to six pairs and finish as in note 24.

Owl

Set up as in note 1a at pinhole A *(diagram 84)* working in whole stitch to B, and add one pair

(note 2a). Make the edge stitch and bring the coarse pair into position. Work through the coarse pair and one more pair; leave the runners and take the last pair worked through as new runners and work to hole C (the ear). Tie well back so that the ear will stand out. Work across all pairs to D and repeat as above to hole E. Work three rows before the eyes are worked *(note 13)* and put pins into the holes to keep the spaces open. Change to half stitch for the body (do not cross the coarse thread). Add one pair to make ten pairs and take out one pair at each side before sewing out into the moon *(note 23a)*. Tie in two bunches.

82

83

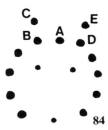

84

Pattern 37b   Owl on Moon (larger size)

(Refer to photograph 85 and pricking 86.) Work in a similar manner to the previous pattern but two extra holes will be worked across the head of the owl. Add one pair at each of these holes before working the holes of the ears.

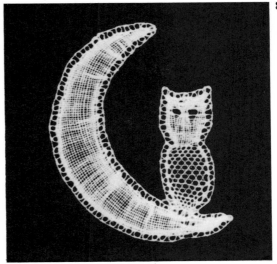

85

86

Pattern 38   Primrose

(Refer to photograph 87 and pricking 88.) Set up with seven pairs at the bottom of the stem. Work in rib up and into the top side of the first leaf, increasing to 11 pairs, and work as for simple raised leaf *(Leaf 4)*. Reduce to seven pairs before crossing the stem to work the second leaf in the same way. A vein can be worked in these leaves. Having completed the second leaf use seven pairs to work up the stem and into the flower, adding a coarse pair *(note 22)* and working the flower in half stitch. The tendril is worked with seven pairs and sewn out into the leaf.

Filling
Swing Leadwork *(filling 30)*.

88

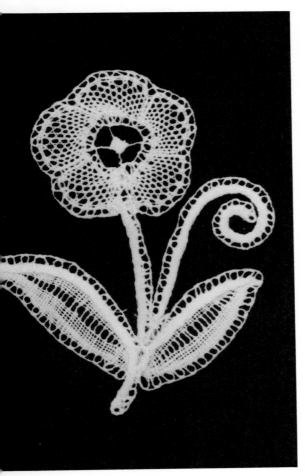

87

Pattern 39 Rose

(Refer to photograph 89 and pricking 90.) Set up six pairs and a coarse pair to work the centre whole stitch section of the flower. Add extra pairs on the outside curve and back stitch at each hole on the inside. Reduce to six pairs and work the outer half stitch petals. Add one pair at each pinhole across the petal to make 11 pairs in all to work the half stitch petals. When the work reaches the completed whole stitch section, sew two pairs of runners into the first hole, tie the outer pair three times and put aside to cut off later. Using ten pairs sewings will now be taken on the inside; complete and sew out. Rib the stem with seven pairs and sew out into the flower. Work the leaf and tendril and sew out into the stem.

Filling
Swing and a Pin *(filling 11)*.

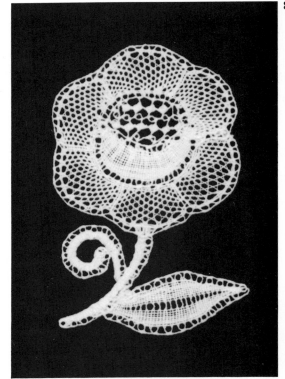

89

90

Pattern 40 Butterfly

(Refer to photograph 91 and pricking 92.)

Antennae, head and body
Work each antenna in rib with five pairs down and into the two top pinholes of the head. Work in whole stitch with the two pairs of runners on the inside to join the two sets of threads. Work one of the other pair of runners to one side where they will, with the edge pair on the plain side, become runners. Make a whole stitch and twist each pair three times ready to work the head. Work the other pair of runners on the inside through one pair towards the opposite side and leave; this pair will now become a downright pair. Twist the pair on the outside three times to become the third runner pair. Weave a coarse pair through the centre pairs as in note 15. Tie one pair of downrights three times and cut out. Ten pairs only will be needed to work the head. Work two rows before the eyes are made as in note 13. Do not weave the coarse pair between

91

92

each section of the body. The half stitch will need ten pairs, the abdomen nine pairs; finish as in note 24.

Wings

Sew six pairs into the lower pinholes of the head and use to rib along the top wing. Add two pairs before the point which is worked as for Leaf 4, increase to ten pairs and work the four pin bud *(note 11)*. The turn into each wing is worked as in note 30a. Bunch the threads, leave one pair aside and use the bunch to roll up to where the pinholes start for the next wing. Sew the pair which made the roll into the opposite hole and tie twice. Use the pair left aside to attach the roll as in note 20g. Repeat for opposite wings.

Pattern 41   Two harebells

(Refer to photograph 93 and pricking 94.) Set up seven pairs for the stem and rib up and into the first leaf. Work in whole stitch as for Leaf 4. Finish the leaf and cross the stem to work the second leaf in the same way. On completion of the second leaf, use seven pairs to work up the stem of the flower. Work around the central petal in rib, adding seven pairs in the three top holes to be put aside to use later for the half stitch centre. After the rib has been worked around the centre, sew in the runners, turn the threads and roll up

(as described in *Leaf 6*) one side of the centre petal. Leave these pairs at the top hole ready for the whole stitch side petal, while working the half stitch down the centre petal. These pairs can then be used to roll up the other side of the centre petal.

Continue along the top of the whole stitch petal adding one pair at each of the first three pinholes and lay aside to use later. At one hole before the point, take the first downright pair and lay aside next to the added pairs. Work to the tip of the petal and tie well back here. Bring the pairs laid aside into position and work across to within one hole of the centre petal. Leave the runner pair here and tie back with the pair laid aside at this point. This tied pair will now become the runner. Work out to the edge and back to the centre bringing in the last pair laid aside. Tie back as before. Reduce to four pairs at the end and sew out. Work the last petal likewise and the second flower in a similar manner.

94

93

Pattern 42   Daisy

(Refer to photograph 95, pricking 96 and diagram 97.)

Leaves

Set up seven pairs for the stem and rib into the lower leaf, adding one pair at one hole before the point. Work the point, turn and work in whole stitch as for Leaf 4 down to the last hole of the top section before the point. Add two pairs, one into the work as a downright and one to lay aside to bring into the work later to fill the gap left here. Work back two pairs, leave the runners, take the last pair worked through as new runners and work to the second pinhole on the outside. Add one pair here. Bring the pair laid aside into position, work through all pairs and sew. Work out to the point, turn, tie and work to the rib, then sew. Reduce to eight pairs before the last hole of this section and repeat as above. Two sewings will be needed in some holes of the rib so that the pinholes on the outer edge can be kept level.

When this half of the leaf is complete, reduce to six pairs and use these to roll to the top; work the second half as the first, but in half stitch using one pair less. Work the second leaf as the first.

Flower

Set up at A *(diagram 97)* with five pairs to rib around the centre of the flower. At one hole before the rib joins, lay in and put aside one pair; join the two runner pairs at A and tie once. Bring in the pair laid aside and use these six pairs to work the half stitch centre. After this has been completed, use the six pairs to rib up the first petal. Work as for Leaf 4. Work in whole stitch using eight pairs. Turn, roll up and work each petal as for Leaf 6. Sew six pairs into the flower for the stem and sew out into the bottom of the leaf.

95

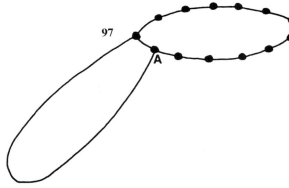

97

A

96

54

Pattern 43   Straight tap leaf

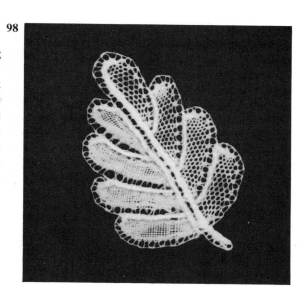

98

(Refer to photograph 98 and pricking 99.) Using seven pairs, rib the stem and the centre of the leaf. Work as for raised leaf with taps *(Leaf 6)* except that it will not be necessary to leave one pair aside at each turn of the tap for use later; this is because each tap is slanting towards the central stem and it will therefore not be such a sharp turn to leave a gap. Taps can be worked in whole stitch on one side and half stitch on the other side as in the photograph.

99

Pattern 44   Curved tap leaf

(Refer to photograph 100 and pricking 101.) Set up seven pairs, rib the stem and the centre of the leaf, as for Raised Leaf with Taps *(Leaf 6)*. Some taps on the curve will need the extra pair put aside to fill any gap here. Complete as Pattern 43.

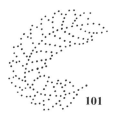

101

100

Pattern 45   Dartford warbler

(Refer to photograph 102 and pricking 103.)
With six pairs, rib the short section at the top of
the wing. Fill with whole stitch and finish in a
position to enable the threads to be used to rib
into and along the base of the lower wing feather.
Fill this with whole stitch, roll and complete
other sections of the wing, working as for Raised
Leaf with Taps *(Leaf 6)*. Set up six pairs and one
coarse pair for the beak, working in whole stitch
into the head. Work the eye as for a snatch pin
hole *(note 14)*. Work a window *(note 12)* at the
neck. Complete top of body and use six of the
pairs to rib up the tail, turn, and with eight pairs
work in whole stitch with two veins. Fill the tiny
section below the tail with whole stitch and sew
out into the wing. Sew in the pairs under the head
for the half stitch part of the body and sew out
into the wing. A few pairs can be laid in ready to
work the leg and centre claw, turn and use the
threads to work the bottom part of the branch.
Work the small claws with four pairs in rib before
the branch is completed, so that they will lay over
it when the work is turned to the right side.

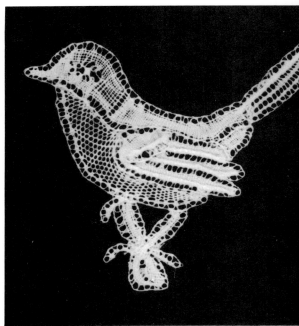

103

Pattern 46   Iris

(Refer to photograph 104 and pricking 105.)
Start at the top of the short veined leaf as in note
1a. Turn at the end of the stem to work up the
flower stem. Take out the coarse pair and use
seven pairs to rib the top of the whole stitch
smaller petal as for Simple Raised Leaf *(Leaf 4)*.
At the end of this petal use the pairs to roll along
the base of the completed petal according to the
section on rolling in Leaf 6, and work the lower
half stitch petal. Carry the pairs forward again to
work the opposite lower petal in whole stitch and
then use the pairs to work the twisted petal.
Change the pinholes to the opposite side to rib

the top. Fill with whole stitch. Use seven pairs to rib around the centre half stitch petal, laying in pairs at the top to work the half stitch later. Roll the rib pairs up to work the other top petal in whole stitch and sew out. Complete the top half stitch petal. The larger half stitch petal must be worked separately. The second leaf is worked in two parts and sewn out.

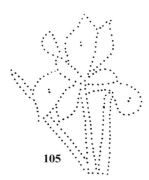

105

Pattern 47 Butterfly

(Refer to photograph 106 and pricking 107.) With six pairs, work the inner antenna in rib. Take the rib forward into one side of the head, changing the pinholes to the opposite side, and work into the thorax. The feet are then worked as for the veins in Leaf 5. Continue the rib into the abdomen and back to the head. Use these six pairs to work the rib up the outside edge of the top wing and across the centre, adding two pairs at each of the top holes as the rib is worked, and also laying aside two of the rib pairs at the last two holes of the rib. Use these pairs to fill the section of the wing with half stitch. Six pairs from this half stitch can then be carried forward to make a roll up the side of the completed half stitch; use these pairs to rib around the lower part of the large centre wing, laying in 20 pairs along the top as the rib is being worked. Use these pairs later to fill the section with whole stitch, working three veins towards the end. Sew out into the thorax, taking six pairs forward to roll and rib the lower wing and laying in and putting aside 16 pairs to work the half stitch. Rib and fill the lower section of the smaller top wing with half stitch.

Rib the second antenna with six pairs, and use

106

these pairs with the few pairs laid aside previously to fill the thorax with half stitch. Rib the top section of the wings with six pairs, laying in pairs at the top as the rib is worked to fill with whole stitch and four pin buds *(note 11)* later.

A small section of the large wing can be filled with No Pin Filling *(filling 4)*.

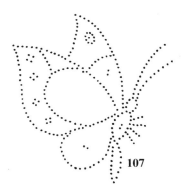

107

Pattern 48 Dragonfly

(Refer to photograph 108 and pricking 109.) Set up six pairs and a coarse pair at the head. Work the top section in whole stitch. On the last hole on each side of this small section add three pairs. Use these three pairs and the original runner on each side to work a rib for the eyes. Work a plait with the remaining centre pairs, i.e. the coarse pair and four downright pairs. The rib pairs and the pairs from the centre plait will now join to work the next section. Make a back stitch at the last hole on each side. Work one pair of runners to the centre and leave them to become a downright pair. Weave the coarse thread on each side to become the third and fifth position at the edge. Tie two downright pairs three times and take them out. Work the next section in whole stitch but do not cross the coarse thread between each section. Take out two pairs on each side

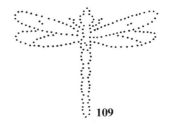

109

before working the half stitch section with eight pairs. Use these eight pairs to complete the body. One section has the runner pair and centre pair twisted twice to make a variation. Finish as in note 24. Work a rib with four pairs for the legs at the top; sew out into the body and use them with two extra pairs added to rib the top wing. Fill with half stitch, turn as in note 30a at the end to roll, rib and work the lower wing as for Raised Leaf with Taps *(Leaf 6)*.

108

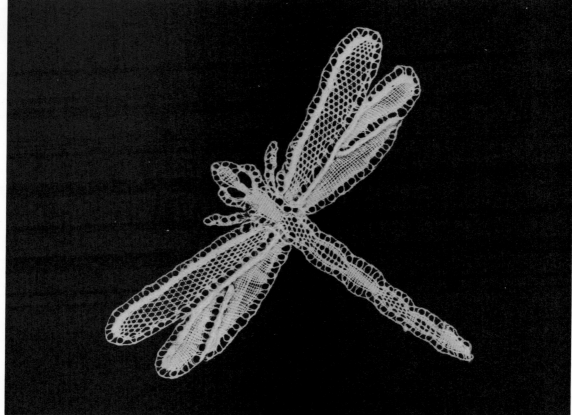

6

Raised and Rolled Work

Pattern 49   Snowdrop

(Refer to photograph 110 and pricking 111.)

Leaves

Start at the bottom of the first leaf with seven pairs to rib up to the turned tip of the leaf. Change the pinholes to the opposite side and rib the lower part of the turned tip. Work as for Simple Raised Leaf *(Leaf 4)* in whole stitch. Toward the finish of the tip, lay aside two pairs at each of the two holes on the rib side before the end of the turn; these pairs will be in position to fill in the bottom part of the leaf. Sew out. To work the other two whole stitch leaves, sew seven pairs into the first leaf so that the top row of pinholes can be worked in rib; work as for Simple Raised Leaf *(Leaf 4)*. For the top centre leaf set up six pairs and a coarse pair, increasing to nine pairs. Work in whole stitch, making a vein.

Flowers

Rib up the stem of the flower with seven pairs, and into and around the calyx with six pairs. Lay in two pairs each side and put them aside to use with the six pairs of the rib to work the calyx in whole stitch. Sew in all pairs and tie twice. The centre three or four pairs can now be used to work the rib around the centre petal. Add pairs into the rib to make seven pairs; lay in and put aside 14 pairs as the rib is worked at the top holes (two pairs at each of the five centre holes). These pairs will be used to fill the centre petal with half stitch later. Complete the rib and sew out into the

111

calyx, but do not cut off the threads until the half stitch has been worked and sewn out. Sew in pairs for the two side petals to use with the few pairs that were left when sewing out the calyx threads. Rib along the outside of these petals and fill with whole stitch, using 14 pairs. Sew out. The tiny rib between the petals is worked with six pairs, a single Swing Leadwork *(filling 30)* is made in the spaces between.

110

Pattern 50   Sweet pea

(Refer to photograph 112, pricking 113 and diagram 114.)

Leaves

Rib the centre vein of the complete leaf first as for Leaf 5. Towards the end, put aside three pairs from the rib and add two pairs to use for the half stitch side of the leaf which is worked first. Add one coarse thread to use for the outer edge of the leaf, removing one downright thread. Four of the rib pairs can be put aside and brought in at the finish of the whole stitch side to work the short stem. Work the half stitch, and sew one runner into the top hole of the side veins as they are reached. Turn at the top of the leaf and work in whole stitch. Work the stem and sew out into the side of the completed leaf. Work the second leaf in a similar manner.

Flowers

Work the central large flower first. Rib with seven pairs from the point around a lower petal. Add in pairs to put aside; use them with the rib pairs and fill with whole stitch. Carry seven pairs forward to rib and work the opposite petal in whole stitch. Sew out.

   For the larger top petals, sew seven pairs into a completed petal. Rib around the petal, lay in and put aside 27 pairs at the top to work the whole stitch later. Use the rib pairs to roll up this completed central rib. These pairs are then put aside until the whole stitch has been worked. Near the end of the whole stitch, work a few veins (two twists only). Sew out. Return to the seven pairs put aside, rib round and work the second petal as the first. Rib and fill the smaller petals in half stitch.

Top flower

Work the calyx first *(diagram 114)*. Sew in six pairs at A. Work the stem in whole stitch and continue into the calyx with a rib to the centre point C. Add and put aside one pair at each of the three holes before the point. Turn at C, fill with whole stitch, bring in the pairs laid aside at each rib pin hole, also adding three pairs on the pin side. Take sewings to hole B and work to D,

where three pairs are added – two pairs into the downrights and one pair to put aside. Make up the edge pair, work back two pairs, leave the runner pair and take the last pair worked as new runners to work to hole E. Add two pairs here, one pair to put aside and one pair into the work. Add one working pair at each hole to the point F, and also one pair at each of the two holes before the point to put aside. These pairs are put aside to use after the turn has been made at F. Back stitch on the pinhole side so that hole G will be the last pinhole used before working across all pairs to B – this will prevent a gap appearing at D. Complete the calyx and sew out into the stem. Sew five pairs into the calyx to rib the other small sepal and fill with whole stitch. Sew out. Rib and work the petals of the flower as for the sample shown.

The Bud

Work up the stem and into the bud. Rib the calyx and work this in a similar manner to the calyx of the large flower. Rib the lower side of the top section and fill with whole stitch. Work several rows with veins near the finish. Sew out into the calyx. Rib and work the lower section in whole stitch. Swing Leadworks *(filling 30)* have been worked in the small spaces in this and also the top flower.

The Small Bud

Rib with six pairs around the calyx. Sew out into the stem of the first bud and carry the pairs forward to rib the bud to the tip. Turn and fill with half stitch to the lower point of this top section. Lay in two pairs where the whole stitch will start later. Also put aside one pair at each hole from the half stitch as it is worked to use when the whole stitch is worked across all pairs later. Complete the whole stitch. Sew out into the stem of the first bud and use eight pairs to fill the ribbed calyx with whole stitch. Use these pairs to work the stem. Sew out into the first stem.

Pods

Rib with five pairs around the outside of the sepal. At each of the three holes before the end, lay in one pair, turn and fill with whole stitch. When complete, use six pairs to work a rib along one edge of the pod. Lay in and put aside one pair at each hole from the widest point to the tip. Turn and fill with half stitch using in all 13 pairs. Sew out into the sepal.

Second Pod

Sew five pairs into the first pod and use to rib the inside pinholes of the smaller sepal. Fill with whole stitch. Roll six pairs to be in position to work the second sepal. Work as first sepal and sew out. Sew six pairs into this section to rib and work the second pod as the first.

Tendrils

Work the centre straight tendril from the tip with seven pairs. Work into and fill the centre with whole stitch into which the other tendrils will be sewn. Add two extra pairs and tie well back at the first two holes of this whole stitch. Complete the tendril and sew into the leaf stem. Work all tendrils. All stems are worked in whole stitch using a coarse pair.

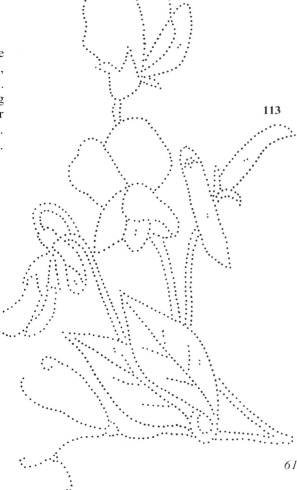

113

114

61

Pattern 51   Leaf sampler

(Refer to photograph 115, pricking 116 and diagram 117.) This sampler incorporates the seven leaves in Chapter 8. Diagram 117 shows: 1. Divided Leaf; 2. Centre Leadwork and Pin; 3. Rib Leadwork Centre and Points; 4. Simple Raised Leaf; 5. Leaf with Raised Veins; 6. Raised Leaf with Taps; 7. Ladder Trail. Work the whole stitch pointed leaf as for Leaf 3. After working the central rib and leadwork centre, work the stem in whole stitch to the point and finish as in note 24. Complete this leaf. Work the Raised Vein Leaf next *(Leaf 5)* and sew out into the stem of the first leaf. The leaf with the Centre Leadworks and Pin will be worked next. Start at the top and work as for Leaf 2. Sew out into the side of the first leaf in two parts using the pairs nearest to the Tap Leaf to turn and work this leaf as for Leaf 6. Sew six pairs into the side of Leaf 2, add a coarse pair and work as for Leaf 1. To work the Simple Raised Leaf *(Leaf 4)* sew seven pairs into the whole stitch side of the divided leaf. Rib up the side, working as for Leaf 4, and having turned at the top, complete as for Leaf 7.

115

Pattern 52   Buttercup spray

(Refer to photograph 118 and pricking 119.)

Leaves

Set up with seven pairs to work a rib to the top of the lower half stitch leaf. Work as for Simple Raised Leaf *(Leaf 4)*, adding pairs as the shape widens. Reduce pairs and sew out into the stem. Set up with seven pairs at the top central pinhole on the small divided leaf next to the first half stitch leaf. Work in rib to the bottom of the leaf, add a coarse thread on the outside edge of the divided leaf. Back stitches will be needed on the last two holes to turn and work the half stitch side of the leaf. Reduce to five pairs to turn the tip of the leaf. Work down the whole stitch side, adding pairs as necessary and sewing out at the base of the leaf. Seven pairs can be laid in as this whole stitch side is being worked to use later for the rib of the small leaf on the side. Work as for Leaf 4 and sew out.

The large central Divided Leaf is worked as the last leaf except that the rib pairs will be sewn to the edge of the first leaf and the threads turned to work up the half stitch side. Add and reduce pairs

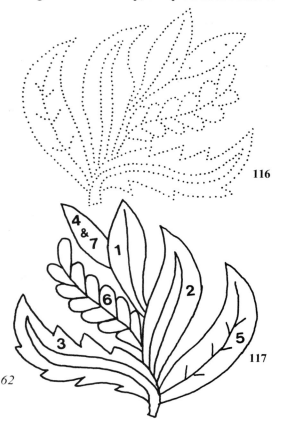

116

117

as necessary. Work the small half stitch leaf and when sewn into the centre leaf, use the threads to turn, roll and rib the curved whole stitch section.

The bottom section of the turned tip leaf is worked exactly as the central leaf. Pairs may be laid in ready to use for the tip as the lower part is being worked. Work the small half stitch leaf opposite as for Simple Raised Leaf (Leaf 4).

The remaining whole stitch leaves will be worked as for Simple Raised Leaf (Leaf 4) working a four pin bud (note 11).

Flower

Use seven pairs to rib the centre of the top half stitch flower, finishing at a point where the threads can be carried forward, working as in note 34a (diagram 207a), and complete the half stitch petals. When the flower is completed, some of the threads on the outside can be carried forward and used to work the stem. The last small whole stitch leaf can be worked now.

Bud

The lower flower bud: sew six pairs into the half stitch leaf to work the stem of the lower bud.

Change to rib to work around the centre petal of the bud, laying in pairs along the top as the rib is being worked to use later for the half stitch filling. Cross over the first rib and work the nearest sepal. Work as for Simple Raised Leaf (Leaf 4). Use these threads to roll, rib and work the side petal, which is also worked as for Simple Raised Leaf (Leaf 4).

Cross the threads once more to work the opposite sepal and petal. Sew out. Work the half stitch in the centre petal and sew out. Sew six pairs into the half stitch leaf to work the short braid. Sew out into the stem of the bud. Work the remaining bud in the same way.

Filling
No pin (filling 4).

119

118

Pattern 53 Butterfly

(Refer to photograph 120 and pricking 121.)

Antennae, head, thorax and body
Set up six pairs for each antenna. Work around the circle and join into the first hole as the rib works down to the head. Work the second antenna. Hang two pairs on the single central hole for the head and twist each pair twice. Weave the coarse pair through the centre pairs *(note 22)* and tie out three pairs from the rib downrights. Work the head in whole stitch using 12 pairs and after three rows work the eyes as in note 13. When the head is completed cross the coarse thread *(note 15)* and work the thorax in half stitch with 12 pairs. Cross the coarse thread *(note 15)* and work the abdomen with a vein. Finish as in note 24.

Top Wing
Sew seven pairs into the side of the thorax and rib the top whole stitch section of the wing. Turn and work back increasing to ten pairs. Turn as note 30a into the whole stitch section at the bottom of the top wing and rib this with seven pairs. Turn as note 30a and fill with whole stitch. Work down to the thorax and sew out. Sew in seven pairs and work the rib of the half stitch section of the top

wing. Turn and fill with half stitch increasing to 18 pairs. Rib up the outside of the wing with six pairs. Lay in and put aside three pairs, as well as two pairs from the rib and sew the remaining four pairs into the half stitch section. Turn and work back in whole stitch with veins, increasing to 14 pairs at the widest part. Use six pairs at the finish of this section to rib the next section and fill with whole stitch working a four pin bud *(note 11)*. Sew out *(note 23a)*.

Lower Wing
Set up eight pairs and a coarse pair at the point *(note 1a)* and work the half stitch section of the lower wing, increasing to 17 pairs. Take out pairs as the section narrows and sew into the side of the thorax.

121

For the raised taps in the lower wing, sew six pairs at the tip of the half stitch section and work the three wider taps using 12 pairs *(Leaf 6)*. Sew two taps into the half stitch and the last tap out into the side of the thorax. Sew six pairs into the top of the half stitch section again and roll these pairs up the side of the first rib. Work the remaining four taps, all in whole stitch, and sew out. The outer edge of this wing is ribbed with seven pairs and filled with whole stitch using 12 pairs. Work the opposite wings in a similar manner.

Filling
Toad in the Hole Variation *(filling 2)*.

120

Pattern 54   Chrysanthemum

(Refer to photograph 122 and pricking 123.)

Stem and flower

Start at the base of the stem, working in whole
stitch using a coarse pair. When the large leaf is
reached, put aside several of the pairs plus the
coarse pair to use for the remainder of the main
stem later. With seven pairs rib up the centre of
the large leaf, tie the threads in a bunch and bow
off the bobbins leaving the ends long. Continue
working the main stem to reach the top flower.
Take the coarse pair out and rib the lower left
centre whole stitch petal and complete according
to instructions for Simple Raised Leaf *(Leaf 4)*.
Carry the pairs forward and upward to work the
next whole stitch petal on the same side. The
pairs will need to be rolled for some petals while
others will need ribs. Work all petals on the
opposite side – rib and roll as necessary. The
other flower is worked in a similar manner.

Leaves

First work the leaf where the rib has already been
made and the threads put aside. Start at the top
hole with six pairs and a coarse pair. On reaching
the centre top hole of the rib, sew the runner pair
into the hole and also sew one pair of the centre
downrights into the same hole to become the
second runner pair for the other side of the leaf.
Work the points as for Leaf 3. Complete and sew
out into the main stem. To work the other large
leaf, rib from the top centre pinhole. Sew out into
the stem. Bow off the bobbins but leave the ends

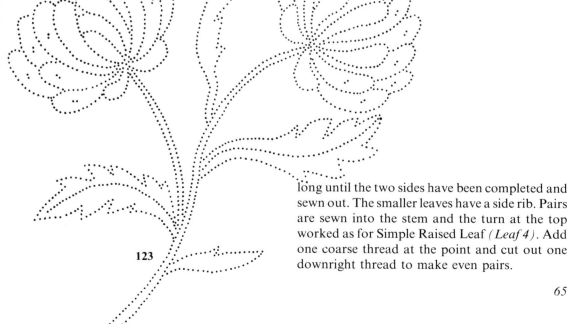

long until the two sides have been completed and
sewn out. The smaller leaves have a side rib. Pairs
are sewn into the stem and the turn at the top
worked as for Simple Raised Leaf *(Leaf 4)*. Add
one coarse thread at the point and cut out one
downright thread to make even pairs.

123

Pattern 55 Azalea

(Refer to photograph 124 and pricking 125.)

Leaves

The vein of the lower large leaf on the right should be worked first as for Leaf 5. Carry the rib pairs forward to work the single small leaf as for Simple Raised Leaf *(Leaf 4)*. At the top of the leaf add one coarse thread, take out one downright thread to make even pairs. Complete and take the pairs back into the first leaf, working whole stitch and four pin buds. 18 pairs will be needed at the widest part of the leaf. Attach by sewing one of the runners at the top hole of each vein as they are reached. Complete and sew out. Bow off the bobbins but leave the ends of the threads long until the turn of the rib for the second leaf has been made. Work up the side with the four pin buds and after the turn at the top, rib and work the turned tip. Lay in and put aside a few pairs to work the remaining whole stitch. All the long ends can now be cut off. Work the other leaf with raised veins.

Flower

Start with the top flower. Set up six pairs and work the centre stamen in rib; continue with rib into and around the lower whole stitch petal. Sew and join the rib, then use six of these pairs to work up a second stamen. Having worked the top of the stamen, take out two pairs, sew out and bunch the threads. This tiny bunch of threads should not show if tied firmly back to the pinholes. Set up eight pairs and one coarse pair at the top of the petal on the left of the stamen. Work in half stitch increasing to 17 pairs; keep the half stitch fairly thick so that when the centre is started it will not leave a gap. Having reached the top centre pinhole, take two pairs of the centre downrights, make a whole stitch, work the runner pair through one of these pairs, then add the top pin. Take the second centre pair as runners and work out to the edge and back to the centre, working through the original runners. The two runners actually cross and work out to opposite sides. Add a pin at the first hole on each side of the centre pinhole and work as for Leaf 2. Sew out. Use a few of the pairs to work up the third stamen; the remaining pairs can be put aside and used later. Work the next petal in a similar manner. Sew out and use some of these pairs with the pairs left from the first petal to fill the lower petal with whole stitch. Sew out. The two remaining petals are worked and sewn out into the lower whole stitch petal. Work the

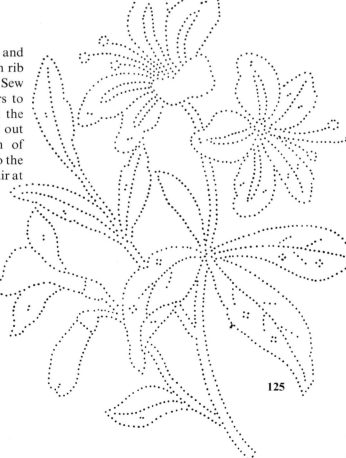

125

second flower. Rib around the calyx of the larger bud with six pairs and begin at a point where, when joined by sewing, the pairs can be carried forward to rib the centre petal. Add one extra pair for this rib. Lay in 18 pairs along the top of the petal and put them aside to use later when the petal is filled with whole stitch. Sew out the rib pairs, leaving the threads long so that they can be lifted when the sewings are taken here. Use the pairs laid in to work the petal, the calyx and the short stem. Sew out. Rib and fill the side petals with half stitch. Work the smaller bud in a similar manner. The remaining leaves are worked as for Leaf 1. Complete all stems.

Pattern 56   Lily

(Refer to photograph 126 and pricking 127.)

Flowers

This spray is started with the large flower, working around the calyx with a rib. Work one side and fill the whole stitch and then use seven pairs to work the rib around the second side. Fill with whole stitch. The spots in this pattern are worked as in note 32. Three of the petals are worked with turned tips. Work the whole stitch petal which crosses the main stem first. Sew seven pairs into the calyx, rib the bottom section and fill this with whole stitch, but lay in and put aside seven pairs ready to work the tip of the petal later, as for Leaf 4. Sew out into the calyx.

The other large petal is made by working the rib from the calyx, changing the pinholes to the other side for the rib of the turned tip and fill in with whole stitch, as for Simple Raised Leaf *(Leaf 4)*. Pairs may be laid in and put aside on the outer curve as the rib is worked to use for the whole stitch later, adding the spots as in note 32.

The stamens are worked next. Starting from one point of the long stamen and finishing as in note 24. The pairs from the three short stamens can be used to work up the stems and sew out into the calyx. The pairs for the stem of the long stamen are worked to the calyx, turned, then using seven pairs work the rib of the lower half stitch turned tip petal. Rib to the tip and change the pinholes to the opposite side. Rib the tip and work as for Simple Raised Leaf *(Leaf 4)*, taking the threads forward and using them to fill in the half stitch lower part of the petal. The remaining petal is worked in a similar manner. Fill the spaces between the stamens with a rib and whole stitch. The buds are worked as the flower petals. The long bud has Swing Leadworks *(filling 30)* worked in. The centre of the opening bud is worked as for Leaf 2.

Leaves

The lower leaves are worked as for Leaf 1; some have turned tips and are worked as for Simple Raised Leaf *(Leaf 4)*. Starting with the central stem, sew six pairs into a petal of the flower and work in whole stitch down into the left lower leaf.

In this way all four leaves can be worked without sewing out, as pairs can be carried across the stem for each leaf. The small leaves are Simple Raised Leaves *(Leaf 4)*, working up the main stem and into the rib for these.

127

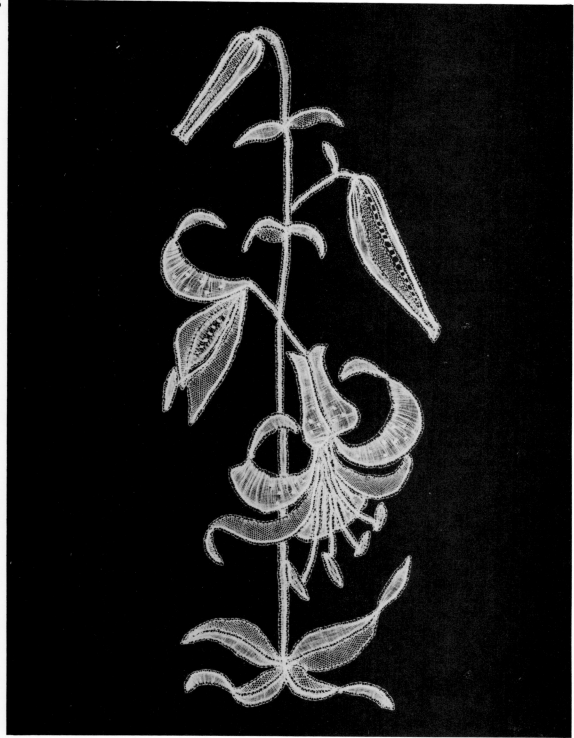

Pattern 57 Floral spray

128

(Refer to photograph 128 and prickings 129a,
129b, 129c, 129d.) This spray is also suitable for a
wedding veil or a central panel of a christening
robe. It is worked on four separate patterns and
the sections joined later. Pricking 129a is worked
first. Side flowers and spray of leaves 129b are
then worked, followed by the central flower.
Pricking 129b should then be turned over to
work on the reverse side so that both parts will
match. Join to 129a by working the stems
between. Pricking 129c can now be worked. This
will join to the centre flower by working the two
connecting stems. Pricking 129d, the small top
section, will sew out into the top rose. The
working of this spray is quite straightforward.

Fillings
No Pin *(filling 4)*; Swing and a Pin *(filling 11)*.

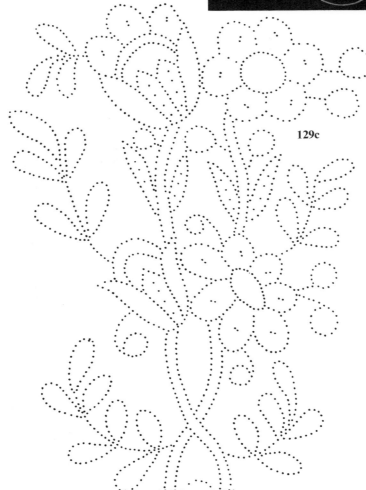

129c

70

129b

129d

129a

71

Pattern 58 Poppy

(Refer to photograph 130, pricking 131 and diagram 132.)

Flower

Set up seven pairs at A and work in rib along the top of the lower petal of the flower. Lay in five pairs at B to work the short rib around the centre of the flower. The five pairs can be sewn out at C after the main rib has passed this point, but leave these ends long until the whole stitch has been worked in the petal. When the rib reaches the widest point at the bottom of the petal, lay in two pairs at each hole and put aside to use later to work the whole stitch. Put aside one pair from the rib at each of the two holes before the join at A, leaving five pairs to turn and use to start the whole stitch. 26 pairs will be needed at the widest part of this petal; gradually reduce the pairs and when complete, use seven pairs to rib around the top centre petal. Lay in 36 pairs along the top as

130

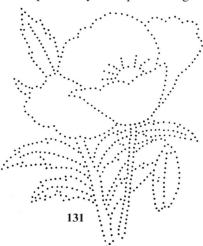

131

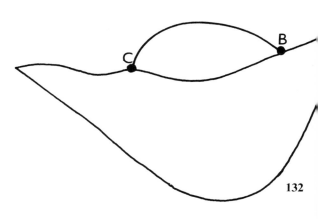

132

the rib is worked and put them aside to fill the petal with whole stitch later. The seven pairs used for the rib can be sewn and turned to roll up the side of the rib of the first petal, and then left in position ready to work a side petal. Work the whole stitch in the centre petal with a few small veins in the centre. Sew out all pairs and use some to roll, rib and work the second side petal. A few of the centre pairs can be used to work the No Pin filling *(filling 4)* in the flower. Work the stems

from the base and sew out into the flower. Rib the bud stem with seven pairs, work around the calyx with five pairs, then fill with whole stitch. Rib and work the bud.

Leaves

These have a centre vein. Work the vein from the top, sew into the stem and turn to work the whole and half stitch as for Leaf 1, using a coarse thread on the outer edge. Sew into the rib.

Pattern 59   Orchid

(Refer to photograph 133 and pricking 134.)

Leaves

Set up seven pairs at the base of the lower leaf and rib up on the inside. At the bottom of the turned tip of the leaf, change the pinholes to the opposite side and rib the bottom of this turned tip. Work this as for the Simple Raised Leaf *(Leaf 4)*, but lay aside only one pair before the top. When the whole stitch is worked, the shape widens on the pinhole side and extra pairs are added here, making ten pairs. Working towards the base of the turned tip, lay aside four pairs on the rib side to use later with the remaining pairs when working the lower half of the leaf in whole stitch (12 pairs will be needed for this section). Sew out. Work the second leaf likewise and increase to nine pairs. The turned tip leaf will only need seven pairs for the whole stitch tip, and the wider leaf 16 pairs. At the widest point sew out into the first leaf.

Flower

Set up six pairs to work the centre rib and work the stamen as in note 33a. When the rib is finished and joined, the pairs are now in position to work around the top centre half stitch petal. Rib with seven pairs around this petal. Lay in and put aside 12 pairs at the top of the petal to work the half stitch later. When the rib has been made, use the seven pairs to rib along the lower side of one of the whole stitch petals. Work as for Leaf 4, increasing to 15 pairs and when complete, sew out. Work the half stitch in the top centre petal. Sew out all the pairs on one side, while seven pairs on the other side can be carried forward and used to work the second top whole stitch petal as the first. When this second petal is completed, use the pairs to roll up the side of this petal to work the first large whole stitch petal. As the rib is worked around the larger whole stitch petal, lay in and put aside 22 pairs to use later to work the whole stitch with veins. On the top seven holes add two pairs at each hole. Sew to the centre and carry forward seven pairs to rib the second large whole stitch petal. Rib a few holes and put aside while the 22 pairs work the first

133

large petal. Use some of these pairs to turn and roll up the side of the wide petal to rib the lower centre petal, adding 14 pairs at the top as the rib is being worked. Put these aside to work the whole stitch later. After the rib has been made, use the pairs to make a roll along the side of the other wide petal to match the opposite side. Sew out. Leave the ends long until the whole stitch has been worked and sewn out. Work the short flower stem with six pairs and one coarse pair. The centre of the flower has one small Swing Leadwork *(filling 30)*.

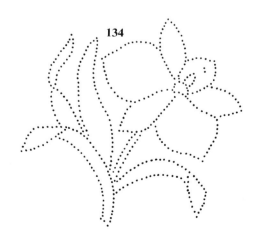

134

Pattern 60 Fuchsia

(Refer to photograph 135 and pricking 136.)

Flower

With seven pairs rib around the underskirt of the blossom; lay in and put aside the pairs to use later for the half stitch. Roll and work the second section, sew out the rib pairs and use the pairs from the half stitch to rib along the bottom of a side petal. Fill with whole stitch, following the instructions for Simple Raised Leaf *(Leaf 4)*. Put these pairs aside and rib the centre petal from the top. Sew these pairs out into the underskirt but leave the ends of the thread long to cut off later. Use the pairs put aside from the side petal to work into one side of the centre petal. Reduce the number of pairs to turn at the top and work the second half of this petal. When this has been completed, a few pairs can be carried forward to rib and work the second side petal. Sew out. The whole stitch bottom section has a rib and the pairs are sewn into the half stitch section, working as in the instructions for Simple Raised Leaf *(Leaf 4)*.

Stamens

These are worked in rib with five pairs. Work the centre one starting with the circle and sew out into the flower. The other two are worked as Stamen b *(note 33)*.

Leaves

The two leaves above the flower will be worked before the stem of the flower can be made. Set up seven pairs at the bottom centre of one leaf. Rib around the centre and continue along the short stem and into the second leaf. Lay in the pairs to use to fill the first leaf as the rib reaches the bottom. The pairs from the rib when completed can be used to work the whole stitch, adding extra pairs as necessary. Work the windows *(note 12)* as indicated on the pattern. The two small leaves below the flower are worked as for Leaf 5. When the veins of a leaf are not opposite, the two extra pairs do not need to be added. Use the seven pairs from these leaves to work up the stem into the two leaves above. The remaining leaves are all worked in a similar manner. The rib

136

vein from the larger top leaf can be worked into
and around the calyx of the larger bud. Fill with
whole stitch. Rib and roll the bud as shown in the
example.

Fillings
Pin and a Stitch *(filling 12)*; Swing Leadworks
(filling 30).

Pattern 61 Wild rose spray

(Refer to photograph 137 and pricking 138.)

Flower
It is advisable to use a large pillow, as some parts of this pattern require many pairs of bobbins. Work the large centre flower first. Set up seven pairs at the narrow point of the lower petal at the first inner pinhole. Rib along the centre line of pinholes and work as in the instructions for Simple Raised Leaf *(Leaf 4)*. Add and lay aside a few extra pairs several holes before reaching the point. Turn here and work the whole stitch increasing to 21 pairs. Reduce to six pairs to turn at the start into the top section of this petal. Rib along the top section of this petal with seven pairs, turn and fill with half stitch. Sew out. Sew six pairs into the rib of this completed petal for the centre of the flower, adding one pair to make seven pairs to work the rib. Sew the rib out and roll the pairs along the top of the completed petal. Continue in rib around a side petal laying in 48 pairs. Put these aside to use to fill the petal in whole stitch with veins later. Sew the rib out and roll the pairs along the completed rib ready to work the second petal later. Return to the pairs previously put aside and complete the first petal. Sew out into the centre rib. Work the other two petals in a similar manner. 66 pairs will be needed for the large centre petal and 50 pairs for the last one. It is advisable to lay in three pairs at the centre hole of the dip at the top of each of the side petals.

Work the smaller top flower in a similar manner. The centre rib of the half stitch flowers is worked first using seven pairs. These pairs can be carried forward to rib around the petals, laying in and putting aside two pairs at each hole along the top of the petals to work the half stitch later. When this rib has been sewn to the centre rib, roll the pairs along the completed rib and put aside ready to work the second petal.

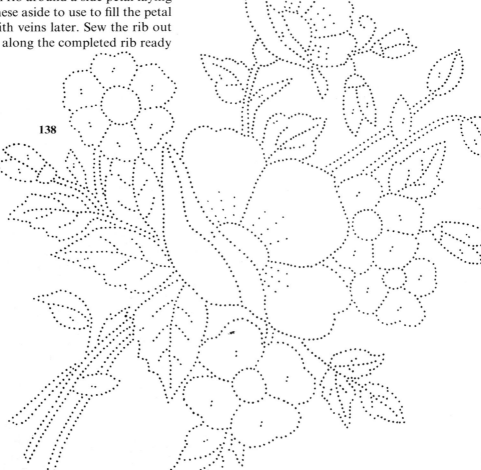

138

76

Leaves
These are worked as for Leaf with Raised Veins
(Leaf 5).

Fillings
No Pin *(filling 4)*; Swing and a Pin *(filling 11)*.

Pattern 62   Lion

(Refer to photograph 139 and pricking 140.)

Head

Start by setting up four pairs for the first tuft of hair on the forehead. Rib with these four pairs and work as for taps in Leaf 6. Work around the first top layer of mane, finishing in line with the bottom of the body. Sew four pairs into the first part of the completed mane to work a second layer of taps, finishing level with the first layer. Work the third and last layer in a similar manner. Sew out. Using four pairs, work the taps around the face and under the neck. Do not work the chin at this stage. Set up four pairs for the eye in the pinhole nearest to the nose and work a rib using the pinholes above the eye; have the holes on the outside edge. Leave these four pairs to use later when working the whole stitch face. Set up with six pairs and a coarse pair as in note 1a on the point of the nose. Work in whole stitch, increasing at each pinhole, and make a vein where indicated by the four holes on the pattern. Continue working in whole stitch until level with the first pinhole of the eye. Sew the runners into this hole and use to complete the whole stitch above the eye. Sew out. Sew a pair of the downrights into the first pinhole of the eye, and use these as runners to complete the lower part of the cheek and eye. The four pairs laid aside may be used now if necessary to fill a gap; then sew out all pairs.

139

For the chin, sew in four pairs, make a roll and join to the lip. Work back in whole stitch, turn and use four pairs to make another roll for the small tap at the bottom of the chin. Sew out.

Body

Start at the tassel of the tail with six pairs and a coarse pair *(note 1a)* and work in whole stitch, increasing and decreasing as the shape alters. Put the bobbins to one side when they reach the back of the body. Sew six pairs into the upper side of the tail to work the top part of the back leg. Add the coarse pair and work in whole stitch straight, adding pairs at each side until the holes at the lowest part of the tail have been used. Working to the body side, work as in note 34a *(diagram 207a)* for about eight pinholes. Work across all downrights continuing to add a pair at each hole on the body side. When the work is level with the threads from the tail, bring these into the work, bringing the spare runners into the work as downrights. Work one row in whole stitch, overlap the central coarse threads for about six threads then lay them back to cut off later.

Continue working with about 47 pairs, adding and reducing where it is necessary. As the whole stitch reaches the mane, sew out the pairs that lie opposite each tap. Start with the inner back leg, working a rib with four pairs, starting on the third pinhole from where the toes begin. Work as for the taps *(Leaf 6)* but at the turn of each tap lay in and put aside two pairs to work the whole stitch leg later. Work up the leg adding and reducing as the shape requires, sewing into the body and along the abdomen. Sew out into the taps of the mane. Working the remaining part of the back leg with taps at the toes and sew out into the tail. Work the front legs, sewing the pairs into the mane to start the rib and working taps for the toes *(Leaf 6)*. Work in whole stitch up the legs and into the mane. The inner front leg has a small roll made at the back and then whole stitch is worked towards the abdomen where the pairs are sewn out. Start the ground on the centre pinhole at one end as in note 1a, and work in whole stitch, increasing to 21 pairs; take out pairs to work around the tail and toes, adding them again as necessary. Finish off as in note 24.

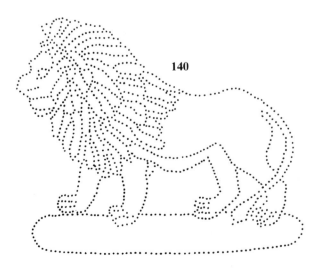

140

Pattern 63 Bell flowers

(Refer to photograph 141 and pricking 142.) As this spray is rather large it is easier to prick the individual flowers first, work them, and then pin them back onto the complete pattern to work in the leaves and stems.

Flower

The two larger flowers at the bottom of the spray are worked alike. Rib from the centre on one side and work outer petal as for Simple Raised Leaf (*Leaf 4*). Carry the pairs forward to rib and work the whole stitch braid around the centre of the flower. Finish with a small section of rib before crossing to work the opposite whole stitch section. Sew out. Pairs are sewn to the whole stitch braid to work the central whole stitch petal first. Turn and use six pairs to roll up the completed petal, and work the side petals in half stitch. Two spaces are left open for fillings later. The small whole stitch petals with four pin buds (*note 11*) are worked from the top and sewn out into the lower petals. Do not bunch the threads. The other three flowers are worked in a similar manner; the half stitch petals at the side are ribbed around the centre and the threads carried around and used to work the half stitch.

Leaves

The leaves are worked as described in Raised Leaves with Taps (*Leaf 6*). Those with centres are started at the base of the stem, worked to the point, and the taps made in the usual way. Work the stems in whole stitch using a coarse pair.

Fillings

Swing and a Pin (*filling 11*); No Pin (*filling 4*); Four Pin (*filling 6*); Swing Leadwork (*filling 30*).

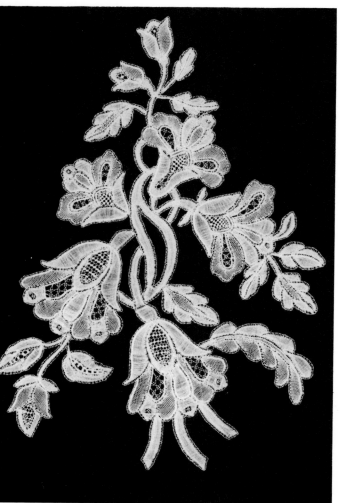

141

142

Pattern 64 Pineapple

(Refer to photograph 143 and pricking 144.) Set up seven pairs for the rib of the centre circle. Join the rib and use these pairs to rib the top half stitch leaf as for Simple Raised Leaf *(Leaf 4)*, but lay in and put aside four pairs at the outer edge from the fourth hole before the point. Lay aside one pair from the rib at each of the three holes before the tip so that the leaf at the turn will not be too thick. Bring into the work the pairs laid aside and take a sewing at every other hole instead of tying back each time. Reduce to six pairs at the end of this leaf and turn into the second leaf as in note 30a. Use 13 pairs for the whole stitch leaf. At the bottom of this leaf roll six pairs up to start the rib for the third and last leaf at this side. Work in half stitch with ten pairs. Sew out. Work the three leaves on the opposite side in a similar manner. Use six of these pairs to carry forward to work the lower circle in whole stitch, using one coarse thread on the outer edge to give body to the work. Add this on a pin with one other thread to make the pair. Add one pair for the outer runners when the pinholes on this side have been reached. Increase to 12 pairs. Two sewings will be necessary at each hole on the inside. Sew in seven pairs for the stem of the tap leaf and work as for Leaf 6.

Work the stem at the bottom with ten pairs.

Fillings

The filling in the circle is No Pin *(filling 4)*. The top half of this pattern is a repeat of the example shown. Work the stem to join them. The larger leaf can be worked as for Leaf 2. The smaller one as for the Simple Raised Leaf *(Leaf 4)*.

143

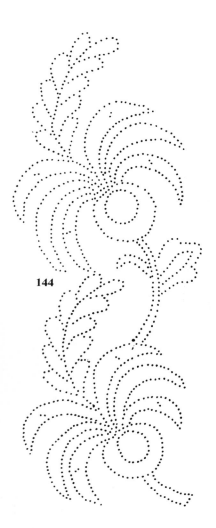

144

145

Put aside two of the rib pairs at each of two holes before the point and use seven pairs to fill the section in whole stitch, working as instructed for Leaf 6. The four lower sections of this leaf will also have a plain whole stitch centre working to the start of each top tap. All taps are worked as for Leaf 6.

Pattern 65   Vine leaf

(Refer to photograph 145 and pricking 146.) This pattern of a vine leaf was taken from an antique Honiton Lace cuff in my collection.

Set up six pairs to work the main stem (a fine coarse pair may be used). Work in whole stitch and add two extra pairs; these two pairs should be taken out again as the stem narrows. Change to a rib for the top tap, laying aside the coarse pair when the rib starts, and cut these off later.

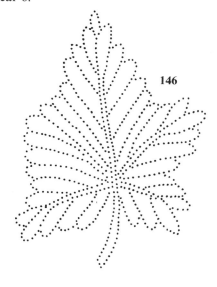

146

Pattern 66   Thrush

(Refer to photograph 147 and pricking 148.) Work a rib with seven pairs from the top along the outside of the large section at the top of the wing; turn and fill with whole stitch. Put these seven pairs aside to use later for the rib at the top of the head, after the wing feathers have been made. Work the small half stitch feathers first and roll between each with five pairs. Rib and roll all whole stitch parts of the wing and sew out. Return to the seven pairs put aside and use them to rib around the top of the head and along the top of the beak. Fill with whole stitch and again put these pairs aside. Work a rib around the eye with five pairs and continue the rib along the top of the half stitch section at the back of the eye; turn and fill with half stitch. Sew out all pairs. Work the inner part of the worm and sew out into the top part of the beak. The lower part of

the beak can now be worked. Take the pairs across the worm and continue into the body – use one coarse thread on the outside, take out the inner coarse thread and one other thread. Back stitch well on the outside and when the eye has been reached, two pairs will need to be sewn into every hole along the base of the eye for the whole stitch braid. Work across all pairs below the eye to join with the pairs which will have been used to work around the top of the head. Some 30 pairs will be needed for the whole stitch body. Work leadworks at random into the whole stitch along the breast as in note 32. When reaching the dividing pinholes at the top of the leg, take two centre pairs, make a stitch but do not twist, lay in and put aside two pairs. These can be used if necessary to fill any gap that may appear when returning to work the second section of whole stitch later. Complete the lower part of the body to a point by the leg, and put aside the pairs as the

section narrows. These can be used later when working the leg.

Continue the upper part to the next row of pinholes of the leg, divide the threads again as before and complete the remainder of the body to the tail. Use a coarse thread along the lower edge of the body. Work the remainder of the leg and rib and roll for the claws. The claws of the second leg are worked first. Put aside a few pairs after each claw has been worked and use them to work the leg. Sew out into the body. The top section of the tail has a rib and is filled with whole stitch. For the remaining tail feathers, sew pairs into the body. Rib and roll all sections, working windows *(note 12)* in the whole stitch. Work the other part of the worm, and one single leadwork for the eye. The branch is worked in half stitch.

148

Pattern 67   Magnolia

(Refer to photograph 149 and pricking 150.)

Flowers

Rib with seven pairs around the centre of the bottom flower. Start at a hole where, when the rib has been completed and joined by sewing, the pairs will be in position to rib around a petal. Lay in 20 pairs as the rib is worked around the top, to fill the petals later in whole stitch. Lay in two pairs at five holes around the point and one pair at the other holes where they will be needed. When the first rib edge has been made and sewn into the centre rib, use the seven pairs to turn and

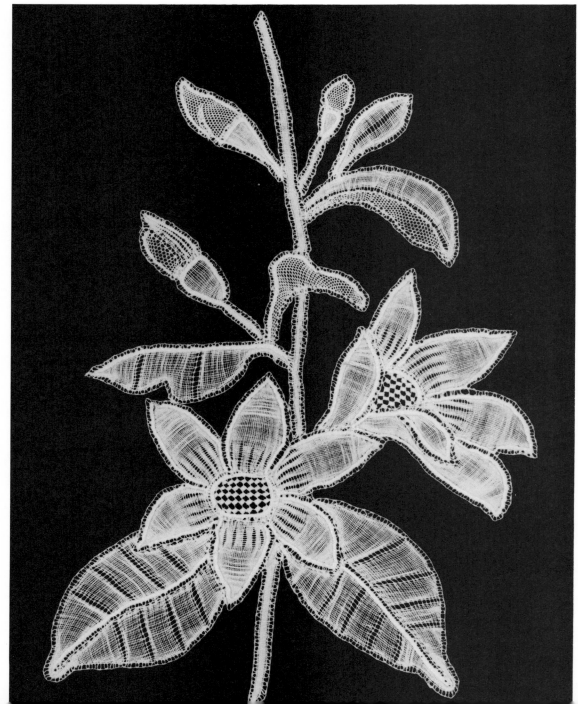

roll along the completed rib to where the pin holes start for the second petal. Leave the pairs aside here until the whole stitch of the first petal has been worked. Twist twice only for the veins at the bottom of each petal. Sew out all pairs into the centre circle rib. A few of these pairs can be put aside to use later to work the No Pin filling (filling 4). Leave one at every hole along the top and also several on one side to use as the runner pairs. Work all petals in a similar manner and sew out all pairs into the centre circle rib. Cut off the bobbins but leave the ends of threads long. The sewings for the filling have to be taken on the same holes where the ends of thread can then be held and these sewings taken more easily. Sew seven pairs into the petal of the first flower to rib the first petal of the second flower. Lay in and put aside the pairs at the top to fill the petal with whole stitch. The pairs from the rib can be carried forward to rib petal two. As this rib is worked, pairs to work the centre rib can be laid in ready; these are used later to rib petal three and

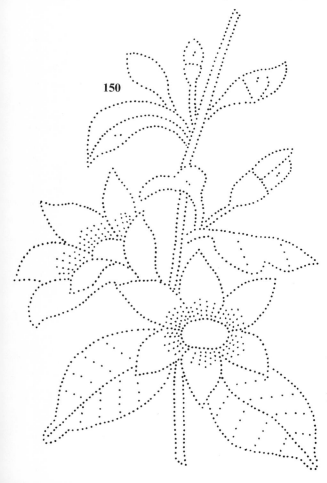

150

sewn out. Return to petal four, rib along the bottom and these rib pairs can be used to rib petals five and six.

Leaves

Set up at the centre top hole with seven pairs and rib the centre vein of the large leaves. Sew into the flower petal, turn and use a few of the pairs with pairs brought forward from the stem. Work stem at the bottom with 11 pairs including a coarse pair. A few of these pairs when sewn can be used with one coarse thread on the outside to work up the section of the leaf to reach the centre vein. Work the windows as indicated on the pattern; 19 pairs will be needed at the widest point of these two leaves, reducing to seven pairs to turn at the top. Complete and sew out into the flower.

Work the centre length of stem next. These pairs will have to be put aside to sew out later when the half leaf and half stitch section above it has been worked. As the rib for the half stitch section is being worked, lay in and put aside one pair along the top of the first curve and two pairs at two holes where the shape dips before the point. These pairs will be brought in as the half stitch is worked; on the inside curve many back stitches will be necessary. Sew out, turn, and use the pairs to work the stem of the bud in whole stitch, changing to a rib for the calyx. Fill with whole stitch and use five pairs to rib one side of the bud and fill with half stitch. Use five pairs to rib the other side of the bud and fill with whole stitch and veins. Work the top part of the stem. The larger top bud has a vein worked from the centre of the bud. Sew into the stem and turn the pairs to rib along the side and across the top of the calyx. Lay in four pairs and put aside to rib the top of the bud after the calyx rib has been sewn out. Rib and fill the top of the bud with half stitch. Sew into the rib across the centre and use the pairs to fill the calyx with whole stitch. Work the smaller bud from the stem into the calyx and fill with whole and half stitch as the previous bud. Work the two remaining leaves, the larger as for Leaf 1, and the other as for Simple Raised Leaf with Vein (Leaf 4).

Filling
No Pin (filling 4).

87

Pattern 68   Iris

(Refer to photograph 151, pricking 152 and diagram 153.)

Flower

Start at 1 and work the half stitch section of the left petal from the top using a coarse pair, increasing to 17 pairs then reducing to six pairs at the end of the section. Take out the coarse pair here. Work in rib along the outside of the narrow whole stitch section 2 and complete and roll the

151

pairs back to the tip to work section 3 in half stitch. Use six pairs to work sections 4, 5, 6 and 7, working as for Leaf 6. Roll and rib section 8 to the top and fill with whole stitch. Sew out at 9. Sew seven pairs into the edge of the petal at 10, rib into and around the two centre points of section 11; lay in the pairs at the top pinholes ready to use later to fill with whole stitch. The rib pairs can be used later to rib the inside of section 12, but leave these pairs aside until section 11 has been filled with whole stitch. The whole stitch pairs can be carried forward to rib the outer section of 13. Complete section 12 and turn as in note 30a to rib the outer edge of section 14. Complete section 13 and sew out. Return and fill section 14 in whole stitch. Use six of these pairs to make a roll up section 15 and change to rib when the top pinholes start; turn and fill with whole stitch but lay in six pairs, putting these aside to use later for the roll along section 17. Complete section 15 and use some of these pairs to roll and rib section 16. When this has been finished, return and roll up section 17 and rib along the top of this section. Lay in one pair at each hole except the last three (here one pair can be put aside from the rib pairs). Fill section 17 with half stitch. Sew in six pairs and rib the centre of petal 18. Lay in pairs at the top pinholes and fill with whole stitch. Sew out at the end, but again six pairs can be laid in ready to make a roll along the rib of section 18 to work section 19. Lay in six pairs at the point where the roll for section 20 will start. Complete section 19 and sew out. Roll, and work as for Raised Leaf with Taps *(Leaf 6)*, sections 21, 22, 23 and 24. Sew in six pairs and use to rib up the outside edge of section 25; turn, and fill with whole stitch. Rib the outer edge of sections 26 and 27 and fill with whole stitch.

Leaves

Work all the leaves from the bottom in whole stitch and sew out into the petals. The top of the leaves begin at the points, and are sewn out into the petals. Do not bunch the threads. To work the stem of the flower, rib up and fill the top section 28 with whole stitch. When complete use six pairs to roll up and work section 29. Use the pairs left from section 28 to rib down the lower edge of section 29. When section 29 has been completed, use six pairs to roll along the line of pinholes which separate sections 29 and 30. Sew out at the base. Rib and fill the small curved section 31 and work section 10 just above in half stitch.

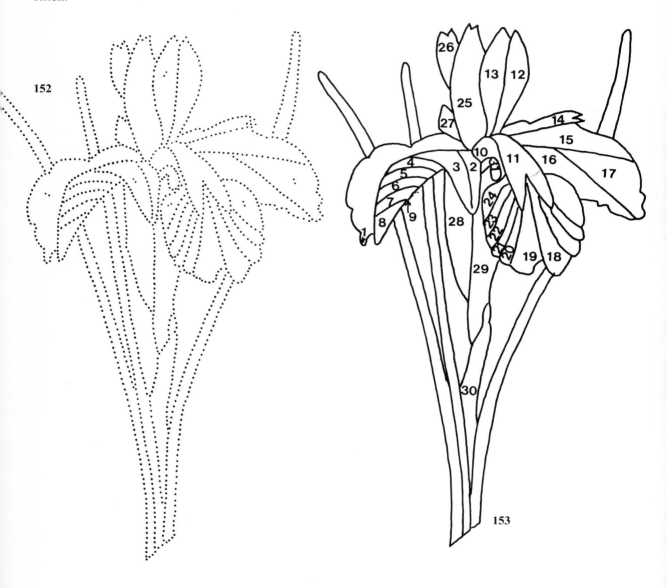

152

153

Pattern 69   Bulrush

(Refer to photograph 154 and pricking 155.)

Large leaves
Set up six pairs and a coarse pair to work the half stitch base, increasing to 17 pairs, finishing as in note 24. All the large lower leaves are worked in whole stitch, or with a vein using 15 pairs.

Cylinders
Set up six pairs at the top of each cylinder and work in rib into and around them, laying in and putting aside two pairs at the first and last two holes. Join the rib and use ten pairs to fill with half stitch. Continue into the stem with rib, sew out. Work all cylinders of the bulrushes likewise.

The smaller leaves at the top and two at the base are all worked as for Simple Raised Leaf (*Leaf 4*).

Pattern 70   Heron

(Refer to photograph 154 and pricking 156.) Set up six pairs and work a rib from a pinhole at the bottom of the body where it meets the thigh. Continue this rib under the head and down the back to the end of the wing. Put these pairs aside. Work the head, starting with the two tufts. Rib these with four pairs each, join and reduce to six pairs to work a rib along the top of the head and into the beak. Turn, and fill the beak and head with whole stitch. Make a snatch pin for the eye (*note 14*) and swing the pairs around to finish at the base of the head. Tie the few pairs left into a bunch, cut off the bobbins, but leave the ends of the threads long, to be cut off later when the body has been made.

Return to the rib pairs put aside and rib around the first section of the wing. Lay in and put aside two pairs at each of five holes to use to fill this section later, when the second and third sections have been ribbed and rolled. Fill each section with whole stitch after the rib has been worked to the top of the wing. Here the threads are tied in a bunch and put aside to bring to the back of the work when the sewing is taken here later. As the threads from each section of the wing meet, sew one pair of runners in the last hole

and leave to become a passive pair; this will help to fill any gap left here. Work the wing in whole stitch with 32 pairs to where the bundled threads of the inner rib have been left. Sew the runners here and also one pair of downrights to become

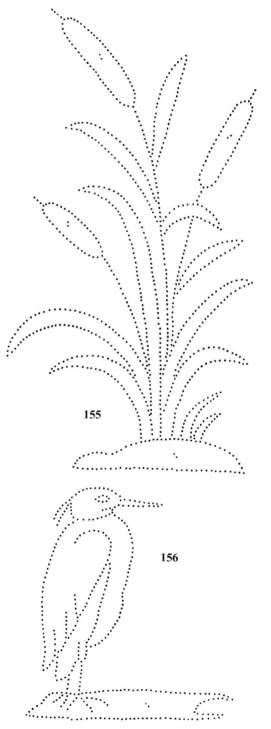

155

156

the extra runner pair needed. Continue working around the top of the wing with 13 pairs, but when the pinholes on the inside are reached, sew in one extra pair to become the edge runner. Work the breast and finish as in note 24. Complete the top of the wing and sew out all pairs into the rib. The claws of the front foot are worked first in rib with five pairs and the three ribs joined to continue the leg. Leave a few pairs aside here and take five pairs to roll and rib the lower end of the second wing. Fill with whole stitch, bringing in the pairs put aside from the leg. Rib the claws and work the second leg.

Work the base in half stitch and join into the base of the bulrushes with a small section of whole stitch.

Instructions for making the dragonfly in photograph 154 are in Pattern 48 (Chapter 5).

Pattern 71 Madonna

(Refer to photograph 157 and pricking 158.) Work the sleeve cuff first. Set up six pairs at the top point by the hand and rib around this section. On reaching the widest point, add one pair at each hole and put aside to make 21 pairs in all, including the rib pairs – put aside one pair from the rib at each of the last two holes. Join at the start and fill the section with whole stitch, gradually bringing in the extra pairs. Reduce to six pairs and use these to rib around the inside of the cuff. Fill this with half stitch using ten pairs.

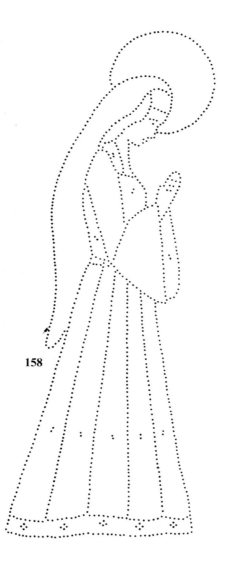

158

Sew six pairs into two holes of the cuff to rib down the front of the skirt and across the base of the first section, laying in two pairs at each hole here. Put these aside and also lay aside one pair from the rib at each of the last two holes. Work across all pairs and fill this section with half stitch using 15 pairs.

Sew into the cuff, turn, and with six pairs, roll to the base of the skirt again and rib along the bottom of the second section. Complete as the first. Work the third section, roll six pairs to the base again and put these six pairs aside to use later. Work the back of the skirt in rib from the base, across the waist, turn, and fill the waistline with whole stitch. Sew out. Return to the six pairs put aside and complete the skirt in half stitch. At the top of the fourth section a few pairs can be put aside to rib around the arm, laying in extra pairs to use to fill this with whole stitch. Add a few veins at random to form a contrast for the arm.

Rib and fill the front and back parts of the bodice with half stitch and also around the face and neck. Rib across the forehead and up around the veil to the lower point, turn and fill with whole stitch. Lay in a few pairs across the top to continue the whole stitch down into the face and neck.

Rib around the hem of the skirt and fill with whole stitch, working the four pin buds. Sew out. With seven pairs rib around the halo adding purls. Use four pairs to rib around the hand and fill this with whole stitch making twists to form the fingers.

157

This piece of lace was presented to Her Majesty Queen Elizabeth II on the occasion of her visit to Exeter Cathedral for the Maundy service 1983. At the presentation, during the reception at the Bishop's Palace, the author had the honour of being presented to the Queen and the Duke of Edinburgh.

7

Fillings

The great variety of fillings is one of the characteristic features of Honiton lace. Many Honiton lacemakers prick their fillings by eye, without the aid of graph paper, sometimes using a ruler as a guide. This makes it possible to fit a filling into a given shape in such a way that the groups of holes are complete at the edges and matching at both sides. An example of such filling worked into a curved space can be seen in Pattern 2. However, to give the student some idea of the size the fillings should be, they are shown here on a grid and should be pricked on *one millimetre graph paper*.

The pairs for the fillings are sewn into the completed braid above and as near as possible to the groups of holes where they will be required, and often more than one pair will need to be sewn into the same hole. When sewing out pairs which have worked a row of filling, they are either tied three times and laid back to be cut off later, or they are brought in again to be used in a subsequent row if they are needed to fill in a widening space.

When a filling has been completed, and all the pairs have been sewn out and tied, the bobbins must be cut off and the ends of the thread trimmed before the pins are removed from the filling. Take out all the pins from the filling.

It often happens that the groups of holes of which many fillings consist are not complete at the edges of the space to be filled. When this happens, work the incomplete group as nearly as possible to the instructions given for these fillings – it is often possible to make a sewing into the

edge of the braid to replace any missing holes. This can be clearly seen in Toad in the Hole *(filling 9)* in the mat sampler *(pattern 17)*.

How to Prick

Transfer the dots for the chosen filling onto tracing paper, lay this over the pricking, and prick through into the space to be filled. Another method is to prick a block of the filling onto a piece of acetate, or used and washed X-ray plate; this is laid over the pricking and pricked through onto the pattern. These pricked 'templates' can be used again and again, providing that the pricking is done carefully, so as not to enlarge the holes in the template.

Filling 1   Diamond

(Refer to diagram 159 and pattern 17: Mat Sampler.) Sew in two pairs above A and two pairs above B. These may be sewn into adjacent pin holes of the completed braid. With the two pairs above A, work a whole stitch and twist both pairs three times. Add pin A between the two pairs. Repeat for hole B.

With each set of two pairs make a narrow leadwork to reach as far as C and D. When both leadworks are complete, twist all four pairs three times and set pins C and D between each two pairs. With the two centre pairs work a whole stitch (No Pin). Twist both these pairs three times. With the two left-hand pairs work a whole stitch, twist both pairs three times and set pin E

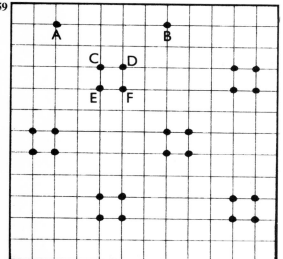

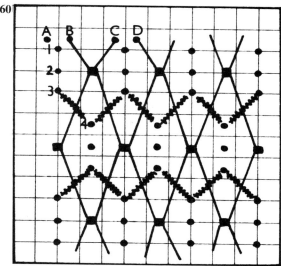

between them. With the two right-hand pairs work a whole stitch, twist both pairs three times and set pin F between them. With the two centre pairs work a whole stitch and twist both pairs three times (No Pin). Each two pairs now work another leadwork to the group of holes diagonally below, where they are joined by two pairs coming in from the opposite direction.

Filling 2 Toad in the Hole Variation

(Refer to diagram 160 and pattern 53: Butterfly.) Sew two pairs into each hole A and D. Sew three pairs into each hole B and C. With the two pairs from A work a bar of three half stitches to reach to I. Do the same with the two left-hand pairs from B. With the two middle pairs of these four, work a whole stitch and one twist and set pin I between them. Work a whole stitch and one twist with each two side pairs. Enclose the pin with a whole stitch and twist, using the two middle pairs. Set pin 2; then again work a whole stitch and twist with the two side pairs. Enclose the pin with the two middle pairs, making a whole stitch and twist. Set pin 3 and work another whole stitch and twist with each two side pairs. Enclose the pin with a whole stitch and twist.

Work a bar of three half stitches with each two pairs and leave. Work another block of three holes as above, using the two pairs from D and the two right-hand pairs from C.

Twist the two pairs remaining at B and C five times each and make a square leadwork with them, twisting them five times again after the leadwork. Work the left-hand pair of the leadwork in whole stitch through the two nearest pairs coming from 3. Leave the leadwork pair aside and with the two pairs from 3 work a bar of three half stitches to reach to 4. Pass the right-hand leadwork pair through the nearest two pairs from the block made with the pairs from C and D. Leave the leadwork pair and work three half stitches with the other two pairs to reach to 4, where another block is made as above.

Filling 3 Jubilee

(Refer to diagram 161 and pattern 16: Sampler 3.) Sew two pairs above A and two pairs above B. Work a whole stitch and three twists with the two left-hand pairs and set pin A between them. Work a whole stitch and three twists with the two right-hand pairs and set pin B between them. With the two middle pairs work a whole stitch and three twists (No Pin). With the two left-hand pairs work a whole stitch and three twists and set pin C between them. With the two right-hand pairs work a whole stitch and three twists and set pin D between them. With the two middle pairs work a whole stitch and three twists (No Pin). Enclose pins C and D with a whole stitch and

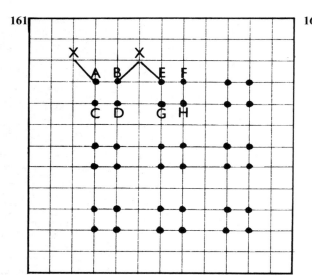

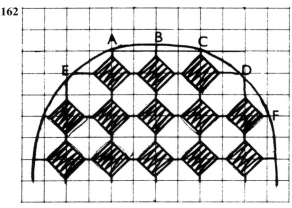

three twists. Work the next group of four holes E, F, G and H as above. Work the two pairs from D through the two pairs from G in whole stitch. Twist all four pairs three times.

Each two pairs are now in position to work the next groups of four holes diagonally below, together with the two new pairs coming in from each side.

Filling 4   No Pin

(Refer to diagram 162 and pattern 17: Mat Sampler.) No pricking is needed for this filling, as the name suggests. It consists of rows of small square leadworks.

Sew one pair into each hole (or if the holes are very close together, into every other hole) in a straight line across the top of the space to be filled, and one pair on the right-hand side (at D on the diagram, usually the next hole slightly below C). Twist all pairs three times. Use the left-hand bobbin from D as the weaver for the first leadwork and take it under, over and back under the next two bobbins (from C). * It is now in the right position to weave the leadwork. When this has been completed, the weaver is again the second bobbin from the left. Twist both pairs three times. This brings the weaver to lie as the outer bobbin on the left. Leave the right-hand pair and work the next leadwork with the left-

hand pair and the pair from B, *again using the same weaver,* which is first passed under, over and back under the two bobbins from B. Repeat from * across the row and after working the last leadwork, sew out the left-hand pair (containing the runner, see *note 20d*) at E. If the shape being filled curves, as in the diagram, sew in a new pair at D and one at F. Twist both pairs three times and work another row of leadworks. The pair sewn out at E may also be brought in again and twisted three times to make an extra leadwork if needed.

Filling 5   Snatch Bar with Leadworks

(Refer to diagram 163 and pattern 17: Mat Sampler.) Sew in two pairs above A and three pairs above B, C and D. If the six holes of the snatch bar are a little way away from the edge at which the pairs have been sewn in, work a whole stitch and one twist with the two pairs from A and the next two pairs from B, and use these four pairs to work the snatch bar as follows. Take the right-hand pair of the four as runners through the other three pairs in whole stitch, twist the runners seven times and set pin A under them. Take the runners back through three pairs, twist them seven times and set pin B under them. Continue working the runners back and forth, twisting round the pins, until all six holes have been used. After the last hole work the runners back through three pairs, then twist the runners and the last pair they passed through once. Work a whole stitch and one twist with the other two

pairs and leave. Work the next vertical snatch **163**
bar, using the two right-hand pairs from C and
two left-hand pairs from D. Twist the two pairs
remaining above B and C six times and use them
to make a square leadwork. Twist the pairs six
times again after the leadwork is completed and
leave. The weaver in every leadwork must finish
in the left-hand pair of the leadwork.

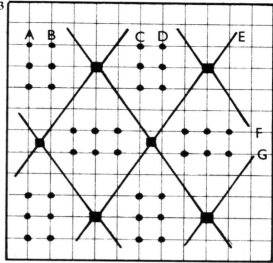

After completing the leadworks, lengthen the
pairs that have made them so that they may be
recognized subsequently. Work a similar leadwork with the pairs from above D and E. The
right-hand pair of the leadwork is sewn out at F
and brought in again. (This pair need not be
lengthened.)

Sew in another new pair at F and three pairs at
G. Four pairs now make a horizontal snatch bar
in the same way as the vertical ones. The pairs of
this snatch bar are now worked through the pairs
of the snatch bar from CD with the leadwork
pairs between as follows. Take the left-hand pair
of the FG snatch bar in whole stitch through the
left-hand pair of the DE leadwork (this contains
the weaver, so work carefully) and through the
four pairs of the CD snatch bar, and leave. Take
the right-hand pair of the CD snatch bar through
the DE leadwork pair and through the three
remaining pairs of the FG snatch, and leave. *
Take the first pair lying on the right of the DE
leadwork pair through the leadwork pair and
through three more pairs to the left and leave.
Take the first pair lying on the left of the DE
leadwork pair through the leadwork pair and
through three more pairs to the right and leave. *
Take the right-hand pair from the BC leadwork
in whole stitch through all nine pairs to the right
and leave it to work the leadwork in the square
below later. Take the first pair lying on the right
of the DE leadwork pair in whole stitch through
the leadwork pair and through four pairs to the
left and leave. Take the first pair lying on the left
of the DE leadwork pair in whole stitch through
the leadwork pair and through three pairs to the
right. Repeat from * to *. This finishes the
crossing.

The four pairs of the CD snatch are now in
position to work the next snatch bar below them,
but before this can be worked, make a whole

stitch and one twist with each two pairs. Similarly, the pairs of the FG snatch bar will work
the next horizontal snatch bar and the leadwork
pair left in position to work the leadwork below
this later, together with another pair coming
from the left.

Filling 6   Four Pin

(Refer to diagram 164 and pattern 16: Sampler
3.) Sew in two pairs above each hole A, B, E, F, G
and H. The four pairs from above A and B work
the first group of four holes as follows. * With the
two left-hand pairs work a whole stitch, twist
both pairs three times, and set pin A between
them. With the two right-hand pairs work a
whole stitch, twist both pairs three times and set
pin B between them. With the two middle pairs
work a whole stitch and twist both pairs three
times (No Pin). With the two left-hand pairs
work a whole stitch, twist both pairs three times
and set pin C between them. With the two right-
hand pairs work a whole stitch, twist both pairs
three times and set pin D between them. With the
two middle pairs work a whole stitch and twist
both pairs three times (No Pin). * The two left-
hand pairs and the two pairs from above E now
work the next group of four holes * to *, and at
the end the two left-hand pairs from this group
meet the two pairs from above F to work the next
group of four holes. Continue down this diag-

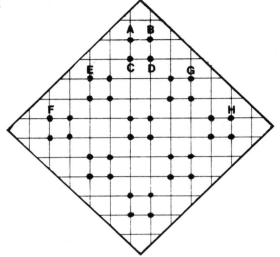

two holes. Sew in two pairs at A and B. Work a half stitch plait with each two pairs to reach to just above C and D. * Use the second pair from the right of these four pairs as runners and take them in whole stitch through two pairs to the left. Twist the runners seven times and set pin C under them. Work the runners through three pairs to the right, twist them seven times and set pin D under them. Work the runners through two pairs to the left and leave. With each two pairs work a half stitch plait to the group diagonally below (four half stitches should be enough), where they repeat the procedure from *, together with two pairs coming from the other side.

Filling 8   Blossom

(Refer to diagram 166 and pattern 15: Sampler 2.) Sew two pairs into the edge of the braid half-way between and above C and A. Sew in two pairs half-way between and to the right of A and B. Work a half stitch plait with each set of two pairs just to reach as far as the group of four holes. The four holes of each group are used to make purls as follows.

Use the right-hand pair of the left-hand plait to make a purl in hole A, * twisting this pair seven times, using the right-hand bobbin to make the loop, and placing the pin under the right-hand thread, pointing to the left, twisting the point over the thread towards you and down into the

onal line until the row is complete; at the end, sew out the left-hand two pairs. Return to the top and work the next group of holes with the two pairs from above G and the two pairs from D. Continue down this diagonal line, using the two left-hand pairs of each group with the pairs left from the previous line of four pins.

Filling 7   Whole Stitch Block Variation

(Refer to diagram 165 and pattern 15: Sampler 2.) Four pairs are required to work each group of

165

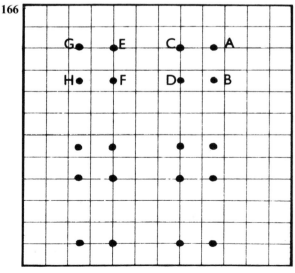

hole. Lift the other thread round the pin from right to left. Twist the pair once. * Make a whole stitch with the two left-hand pairs and twist both pairs once. With the two centre pairs make a whole stitch and twist both pairs once. With the two right-hand pairs make a whole stitch and use the right of these two pairs to make a purl in hole B * to *.

Make a whole stitch with the two right-hand pairs. With the two left-hand pairs make a whole stitch and use the left of these pairs to make a purl in hole C, ** twisting this pair seven times. Place the pin under the left-hand bobbin, pointing towards the right. Twist the point over the thread towards you and down into the hole. Lift the other thread round the pin from left to right. Twist the pair twice (left over right). ** Work a whole stitch with the two left-hand pairs. Twist the two centre pairs once and make a whole stitch with them. Work a whole stitch with the two right-hand pairs. Use the left of these two pairs to make a purl at D, repeating ** to **. This completes one group of holes.

The two pairs between C and D now make a half stitch plait to reach as far as E, where they work the next group of four holes together with the two pairs sewn in above G and E. Put aside the two pairs between D and B. Continue along this row from right to left and after the last group of holes work a half stitch plait to reach the edge, where these two pairs are sewn out. With the two pairs put aside and left hanging below each group of holes, work half stitch plaits to reach the group of holes below. Sew two more pairs in on the right-hand side, and work a half stitch plait to the next set of holes.

Filling 9   Toad in the Hole

(Refer to diagram 167 and pattern 17: Mat Sampler.) Sew in one pair above X and Y and three pairs each above A and B. The pair from X and the left-hand pair from A are each twisted five times and used to make a square leadwork after which they are twisted five times again and left. The right-hand pair from B and the pair from Y are left to work a similar leadwork in the next row. With the two pairs from above A work

167

a whole stitch and one twist. Do the same with the two pairs from above B.

To work the group of six holes, or 'snatch' (as it is called in Devon) use the right-hand pair of these four as runners, and work them through three pairs to the left in whole stitch. Twist the runners seven times, set pin A under them and continue working the runners back and forth to B, C, D, E and F, twisting seven times round each pin. After F has been set, work back through three pairs, twist the runners and the last pair they passed through once and leave them. Work a whole stitch and one twist with the other two pairs and leave. This completes the snatch.

The right-hand pair of the leadwork now works through the two left-hand pairs of the snatch in whole stitch, and is now left for a leadwork in the next row. With the two pairs from the snatch through which the leadwork pair has passed, work a whole stitch and one twist. The right-hand pair of these two becomes the runner pair for the next snatch. This is worked with these two pairs and two more coming in from the other side, either from another snatch or sewn in at the side of the space. The snatch is begun by working the runners through three pairs to the left, twisting them seven times and setting pin G under them. The other two pairs from the first snatch are left to work a snatch in the next row, after a leadwork pair has passed through them. It is best to work this filling in diagonal rows from top right to bottom left.

Filling 10   Italian

(Refer to diagram 168 and pattern 15: Sampler 2.) This is worked without a pricking. Sew in pairs as indicated in the diagram. The pairs across the top are sewn in at every hole, or if the holes are very close together at every other hole. Make a whole stitch and three twists with each two pairs from A, B and C. With the right-hand pair from A and the left-hand pair from B work a whole stitch and three twists. With the left-hand pair from A and the right-hand pair from C work a whole stitch and three twists. Twist the pair from D three times and use it with the right-hand pair from B to work a whole stitch and three twists. Twist the pair from E three times and use it with the left-hand pair from C to work a whole stitch and three twists. Twist the pair from F three times and use it with the next pair on the left to work a whole stitch. Do not twist. Work a whole stitch with the next two pairs on the left; leave these, work another whole stitch with the next two pairs on the left, and so on across the row. The odd pair at the end is joined by the pair from G which has first been twisted three times.

There are now complete sets of four bobbins across the row and complete diamonds have been formed above these. The pair sewn in at H now becomes the runner pair for the horizontal rows dividing the diamonds. Twist this pair three times, * work it in whole stitch through the next set of two pairs, twist the runners three times again and repeat from * across the row, sewing the runner pair into the braid at the other side, after pulling it up well. Ensure the line is horizontal and the pairs through which the runners pass are not twisted.

After sewing, tie the runners once, twist them three times and work a return row as above, again sewing the runners in at the right-hand side into hole H. Occasionally, if the first line is not quite straight, the second sewing may be made into the next hole below H. Again, twist the runners three times and work another row as the first, sewing them out at the end and into the

same hole as the first sewing on that side. This completes one repeat of the pattern. The runners may be needed for the twisted diamond work, otherwise they are tied three times and laid back to be cut off later.

The next set of diamonds is worked as above and is started by working a whole stitch and three twists with each set of four bobbins hanging below the last horizontal bar. The diamond work at the sides will vary according to the shape of the space; the odd pairs at the sides will either be sewn in at the sides, twisted three times, and brought back again to work with any odd pairs, or an extra pair may need to be sewn in, to use with the odd pair at the sides to form extra diamonds in a widening space. There must be complete sets of four bobbins ready before the horizontal line is worked.

Filling 11   Swing and a Pin

(Refer to diagram 169 and pattern 15: Sampler 2.) The holes needed for this filling are pricked in as the filling progresses. The first row consists of leadworks, which are sewn in and made in exactly the same way as described for No Pin (filling 4).

The rows of leadworks alternate with rows in which a twisted pair is worked through the leadwork pairs and pinholes are made, as follows. Sew in one pair at the right-hand edge immediately below the level of the leadworks. Twist this pair three times and work a whole stitch with the pair from the nearest leadwork. Twist both pairs three times. * Prick a hole immediately below the leadwork and set a pin

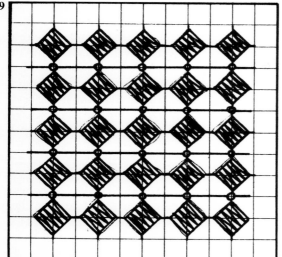

169

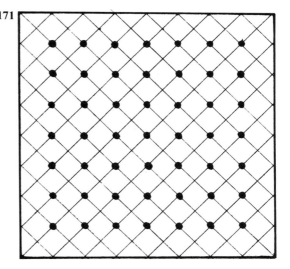

171

into it between these two pairs. Enclose the pin with a whole stitch and three twists. Leave the right-hand pair, and with the left-hand pair and the next pair on the left, work a whole stitch and three twists. Repeat from * across the row. Ensure that the pinholes are pricked in a straight line. Sew out the left-hand pairs at the left side. The next row is a leadwork row.

Filling 12   Pin and a Stitch

(Refer to diagram 170 and pattern 15: Sampler 2.) Sew in two pairs above each hole along the top line. With each two pairs work a whole stitch and three twists and set pins between them, enclosing the pins with a whole stitch and three twists. The pairs now divide to work the holes diagonally below them, the right-hand pair from A and the left-hand pair from B working hole F, etc., as above. The left-hand pair from A meets a new pair sewn in at the edge and twisted three times, to work hole E.

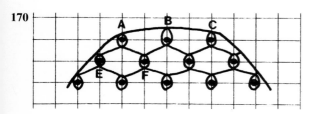

170

Filling 13   Pin and a Chain

(Refer to diagram 171 and pattern 16: Sampler 3.) This consists of a pinhole row and a row made with a twisted pair alternating. Sew in two pairs above each hole along the top. With each two pairs work a whole stitch, twist both pairs three times, set a pin between them and enclose the pin with a whole stitch. Do not twist. This completes the first horizontal row of holes.

Sew in a new pair at the right-hand side, between the row of holes just worked and the next row. Twist this pair three times, and use it as a runner pair to work in whole stitch through the two pairs which enclosed the nearest pin. * Twist the runners three times and work them through the next two pairs in whole stitch, repeat from * across the row and sew out the runners at the end after twisting them three times and pulling up well. The next row is a pinhole row and is worked like the first.

Filling 14   Swing and a Stitch

(Refer to diagram 172 and pattern 15: Sampler 2.) This filling needs no pricking and is similar to Swing and a Pin *(filling 11)*. It consists of rows of leadworks and rows made with a twisted pair alternating. Work the first row of leadworks as explained in No Pin *(filling 4)*. Sew in a new pair at the right-hand edge immediately below the

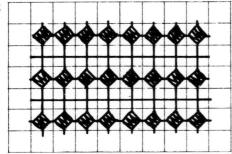

level of the leadworks. Twist this pair three times and work a whole stitch with the nearest lead-work pair, * twist both pairs three times, leave the right-hand pair and, with the left-hand pair and the next leadwork pair, work a whole stitch. Repeat from * across the row and sew out the left-hand pair at the end of the row, after pulling it as much as possible into a straight line below the leadworks.

Filling 15   Trolly Net

(Refer to diagram 173 and pattern 21: Daffodil Mat.) This filling is worked in horizontal rows. (Prick diagonally for a smaller mesh.) Sew in one pair at A, B and C above and between each two holes of the filling. Sew in one pair at D on the right-hand side level with the first row of holes. Twist all pairs two or three times according to the distance between the pinholes and the edge of the braid. With the pairs from D and C work a half stitch, twist both pairs four times and set pin 1 between them. * Leave the right-hand pair, and

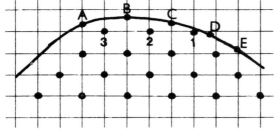

with the left-hand pair and the pair from B work another half stitch and four twists. Set a pin

between these pairs. Repeat from * across the row, using the next pair on the left for each stitch. Sew out the left-hand pair at the end of the row. Sew in a new pair at E, twist it and use it with the pair from 1 to work a half stitch and four twists. Set a pin between these pairs. Repeat from * above. The threads run in a diagonal line from top left to bottom right.

Filling 16   Spotted Net

(Refer to diagram 174 and pattern 35: Leaf Corner.) Work the first row as above. In the next row leadworks alternate with net stitches. The leadworks take the place of one pinhole and are made with the pairs which would normally have made this pinhole. The position of the leadworks may be marked on the pricking before beginning work. The weaver for the leadwork is the second bobbin from the right of the four threads, and it is passed under the next thread on the left, and over and back under the next thread, to bring it into the correct position to begin weaving. After the leadwork is finished, twist both pairs three times, so that the weaver becomes the last thread on the left of the four, and remains the leading thread and weaver for the whole row. The next row is a net row, and in the following row the leadworks come in alternate spaces to the last leadwork row.

174

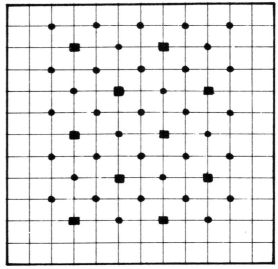

Filling 17 Cartwheel

(Refer to diagram 175 and pattern 15: Sampler 2.) This is often used as a filling for a flower or for a round or oval space. It can be made with six, eight or ten leadworks. Sew two pairs for each leadwork into two adjacent braid holes above the single holes at the top of the filling. With each two pairs make a whole stitch, twist both pairs three times and set pins between them. With each two pairs work a narrow leadwork to the middle row of holes. Twist all pairs three times and set pins between each two pairs into the top row of the holes in the middle. * Leave the outside pair on each side and join all other adjoining pairs with a whole stitch and three twists. * Laying each pair with its original partner (i.e. bringing in the two outer pairs), work a whole stitch and

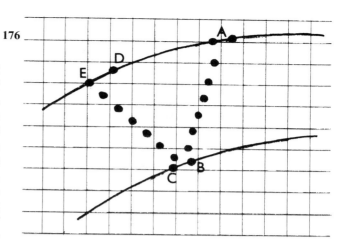

176

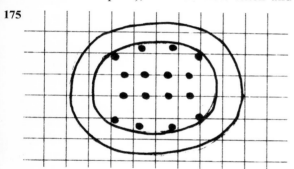

175

three twists with each two pairs, and set pins between each two pairs into the lower row of holes in the middle. Repeat from * to *. Work a leadwork with each two pairs to the holes at the lower edge, twist each pair three times, set pins between them and work a whole stitch. Make three twists if the holes are a little distance from the braid, and sew out.

Filling 18 Purl Pin Bars

(Refer to diagram 176 and pattern 27: Mayoral Edging.) These are made with four pairs which are sewn into two adjacent holes at A. With the first pair on the right, work through the other three pairs to the left, twist the runners once and leave them. * Use the last pair of runners worked through as new runners to work through two pairs to the right. Use this pair to make a

purl on the right side of the bar, twisting it seven times, placing a pin under the outer thread, pointing towards the left, and twisting the pin over the thread towards you and down into the first pinhole. Twist the second thread up round the pin from right to left and pull up. Twist the pair once and work back with this pair through three pairs to the left, twist the runners once and leave them. Repeat from *.

When the bar has reached the opposite braid and the last purl has been made, work the runners back to the left and through to the purl edge again and sew them to the braid at B. Work one whole stitch with the sewn pair and the next pair on the left, leave the left of these two pairs, and sew the right-hand pair at C. Tie this pair once, and use it as the runner to work the next bar. When the last purl of the second bar has been made, work the runners to the plain side and sew them at D. Work a whole stitch with the sewn pair and the next pair on the right, leave the right of these pairs and sew the left pair at E. The purls are usually made on the right side of each bar, but they may be worked on the left, or the left and right on alternate bars.

Filling 19 Brick

(Refer to diagram 177 and pattern 15: Sampler 2.) Sew two pairs above each hole across the top of the pattern. With each two pairs make a whole stitch and twist both pairs three times. Set a pin between each two pairs in the holes below them, and enclose the pin with a whole stitch and three

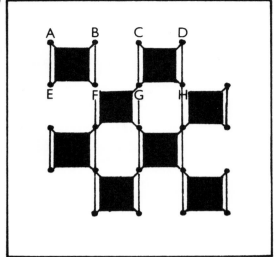

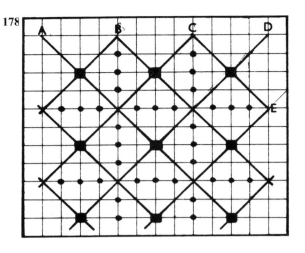

twists. With the right-hand pair from A and the left-hand pair from B, make a leadwork. Repeat with the right-hand pair from C and the left-hand pair from D. Twist all the leadwork pairs three times. With the pair hanging from A and the nearest leadwork pair * make a whole stitch, twist both pairs three times, set pin E between them and enclose the pin with a whole stitch and three twists *. Repeat from * to * across the row with each two pairs (pins F, G, H, etc.). In the next row leadworks are made in alternate spaces (e.g. the right-hand pair from F and the left-hand pair from G make a leadwork) and at the end, the leadwork pairs are joined to the pairs hanging on either side, and the next row of pins is set as above.

Filling 20   Rib Squares and Leadwork

(Refer to diagram 178 and pattern 17: Mat Sampler.) Sew in a pair at A and at D. Sew in six pairs (three into each of two adjacent holes) at B and six pairs at C. Sew in four pairs (two into each of two adjacent holes) at E. With the right outer pair from C and the pair from D, each twisted five times, work a square leadwork. Twist the pairs five times again and leave. Work similar leadwork with the left outer pair from C and the right outer pair from B. With the four pairs left at C work a rib (note 18) with the pinholes on the

right, down the three holes below C. Leave. Work the right-hand pair from CD leadwork in whole stitch through the four pairs from E and leave it to work a leadwork in the space below later. With the four pairs from E work the three horizontal holes in rib with the pinholes on the right.

The pairs from the vertical and horizontal ribs are now crossed, together with two leadwork pairs as follows. Lengthen the two threads of the left-hand pair of the CD leadwork (this contains the weaver so be careful not to draw up the leadwork) and lay this pair over the four pairs of the vertical rib from C. Now lift the four pairs of the horizontal rib completely over the other five pairs. The four pairs of the rib from E are now on the left, then comes the leadwork pair and the four pairs of the rib from C are on the right. Now take the right-hand pair from the BC leadwork in whole stitch through the nine crossed pairs, pull up this pair and the crossed pairs well and leave. Leave the leadwork pair on the right to use later for the leadwork, together with the pair from E. This completes one repeat of the pattern.

Begin the next repeat by working the leadwork with the pair from A and the outer left-hand pair from B. Then the three vertical holes of rib from B and the three horizontal holes of the rib with the four left-hand pairs of those from the last crossing. In these instructions the ribs have been worked with the pinholes on the right of each rib,

but they may equally well be made on the left.
They should always be made on the same side
throughout a filling.

Filling 21   Straight Pin

(Refer to diagram 179 and pattern 15: Sampler
2.) Sew two pairs above each hole across the top
of the pattern; with each two pairs make a whole
stitch, twist both pairs three times and set pins
into the holes between them. With each two pairs
work a narrow leadwork to reach the pinholes in
the next row. Twist the pairs three times and set a
pin between the pairs of each leadwork. Enclose
the pins with a whole stitch and twist both pairs
three times. The right-hand pair from A and the
left-hand pair from B now meet and repeat the
pattern (i.e. make a whole stitch and three twists,
set pin C between them and use them to make
another leadwork). The remaining pairs from A
and B meet a pair coming from each side.

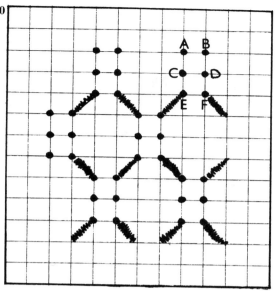

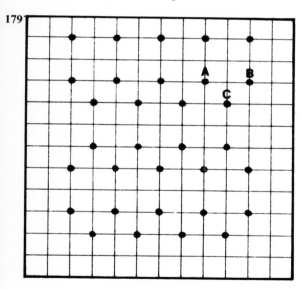

Filling 22   Whole Stitch Block

(Refer to diagram 180 and pattern 14: Sampler
1.) The blocks or 'snatches' are worked as in
Toad in the Hole *(filling 9)*. Four pairs are sewn
in above each snatch hole and a whole stitch and
one twist is made with each two pairs before
beginning to work the snatch. After the last pin

of the snatch has been set, work the runners
through to the outer side once more, twist them
and the last pair they passed through once and
leave them. The other two pairs make a whole
stitch and twist once. The right-hand pair of the
two from E becomes the runner pair for the next
snatch diagonally below and works through
three pairs to the left, then twists round pin G.

Filling 23   Four Pin and Leadwork

(Refer to diagram 181 and pattern 16: Sampler
3.) Sew in two pairs above each hole A, B, E and
F and one pair at each point X. Using the four
pairs above A and B, work the first group of four
holes as follows. * With the two left-hand pairs
work a whole stitch, twist both pairs three times
and set pin A between them. With the two right-
hand pairs work a whole stitch, twist both pairs
three times and set pin B between them. With the
two middle pairs work a whole stitch and twist
both pairs three times (No Pin). With the two
left-hand pairs work a whole stitch, twist both
pairs three times and set pin C between them.
With the two right-hand pairs work a whole
stitch, twist both pairs three times and set pin D
between them. With the two middle pairs work a

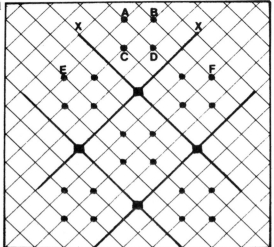

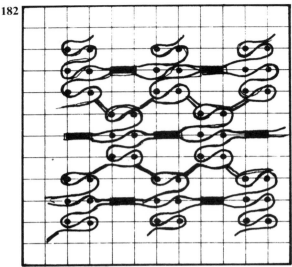

whole stitch and twist both pairs three times (No Pin). * Now enclose pins C and D with a whole stitch. Twist the pairs from X three times and work them in whole stitch through the pairs from C and D, so that they meet in the space below the first group of holes, where they are twisted three times and work a square leadwork. Twist both pairs three times after the leadwork and leave them. The pairs from C and E work the next four pin group from * to *, after which the two lower pairs are enclosed with a whole stitch, and the left-hand pair of the leadwork is worked in whole stitch through the two right-hand pairs of this group.

Filling 24   Toad in the Hole with Wide Leadwork

(Refer to diagram 182 and pattern 16: Sampler 3.) This is similar to Toad in the Hole (*filling 9*), but the leadwork pairs are omitted, the leadwork being made with the runners from adjacent snatches half way through the snatch. Work horizontally as follows. Four pairs are sewn in above each whole stitch block or snatch and a whole stitch and twist is made with each two pairs before beginning the snatch. The runners are the right-hand pair of each set of four and they work back and forth through the other three, as shown in the diagram, seven twists being made round each pin, except the middle pins.

When the middle pin in each of two adjacent snatches has been set, the runner pairs are twisted three times and meet to make a wide, shallow leadwork, after which they are twisted three times again, and each continues to weave its own snatch.

Filling 25   Four Pin with Half Stitch Bars

(Refer to diagram 183 and pattern 2: Shepherd's Crook.) This is used to fill a long narrow space, being composed of groups of four pins, the pairs being attached to the edges of the braid between groups of holes. Sew two pairs into the braid on each side, diagonally above the group of four holes, then work a half stitch plait with each set of two to form a bar to reach the group of holes. * The last stitch of the bar should be a whole stitch, each pair being twisted three times before pins A and B are set between them. With the two middle pairs, work a whole stitch and three twists (No Pin). With the two left-hand pairs, work a whole stitch and three twists, and set pin C between them. With the two right-hand pairs, work a whole stitch and three twists, and set pin D between them. With the two middle pairs, work a whole stitch and three twists (No Pin). Each two pairs now work a half stitch bar to reach to the edges of the braid half way between the sets of holes, where they are sewn, tied once (to hold the

106

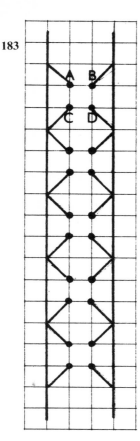

183

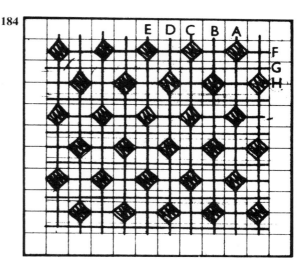

184

bar firm), and then used to work a bar to the next set of holes. Repeat from *.

Filling 26   Devonshire Cutwork (Swing and a Stitch Variation)

(Refer to diagram 184 and pattern 16: Sampler 3.) No pricking is needed. Sew in one pair at every hole or, if the holes are close together, at every other hole, across the top of the space, and one pair on the right side at F, one hole below A. Twist all pairs three times. The left-hand bobbin of the pair from F is the weaver for the leadwork. * It is taken under the next thread on the left and over and back under the next thread, to bring it into the right position to begin weaving a small square leadwork. When this is finished and both pairs have been twisted three times, the weaver is the outer thread on the left of these four. Leave the right-hand pair and with the left-hand pair and the pair from B work a whole stitch and three twists. Pull up the stitch carefully. Leave the

right-hand pair and with the left-hand pair and the pair from C make another leadwork, using the same weaver as for the previous leadwork. This is the second thread from the right of these four. Repeat from * across the row, sewing in the pair which has woven across at the end. For the next row a new pair is sewn in at G, and this is twisted three times. Work a whole stitch and three twists (both pairs) with each pair across the row, after which it is pulled up carefully into a straight line and sewn out on the other side. In the following row the leadworks are made with the pair which made a stitch in the first row, so that they come in alternate spaces and a new pair is sewn in at H to work this row.

Filling 27   Devonshire Cutwork Variation

(Refer to diagram 185 and pattern 14: Sampler 1.) No pricking is needed. Sew in one pair at every hole or, if the holes are close together, at every other hole, across the top of the space, and one pair on the right side at F, one hole below A. Twist all pairs three times. The left-hand bobbin of the pair from F is the weaver for the leadwork. * It is taken under the next thread on the left and over and back under the next thread, to bring it into the right position to begin weaving a small square leadwork. When this is finished and both pairs have been twisted three times, the weaver is

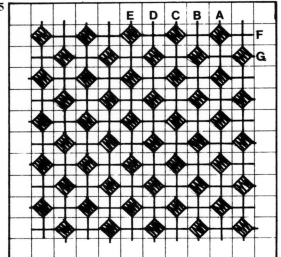

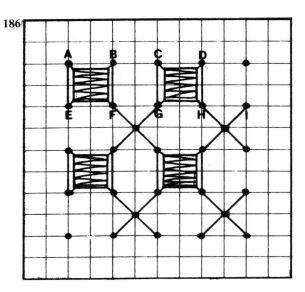

the outer thread on the left of these four. Leave the right-hand pair and with the left-hand pair and the pair from B, work a whole stitch and three twists. Pull up the stitch carefully. Leave the right-hand pair and with the left-hand pair and one pair from C make another leadwork, using the same weaver as for the previous leadwork; this is the second thread from the right of these four. Repeat from * across the row, sewing in the pair which has woven across at the end. For the next row a new pair is sewn in at G, and in this row the leadworks are made with the pair that made the whole stitch, so that they come in alternate spaces, with a whole stitch made between the leadworks. Repeat these two rows to fill the space.

Filling 28   Brick Variation

(Refer to diagram 186 and pattern 33: Fan Corner.) Sew two pairs above each hole across the top of the pattern. With each two pairs make a whole stitch and twist both pairs three times. Set a pin between each two pairs in the holes below them, and enclose the pin with a whole stitch and three twists. With the right-hand pair from A and the left-hand pair from B, make a leadwork. Repeat with the right-hand pair from C and the left-hand pair from D. Twist all the leadwork pairs three times. With the pair hang-

ing from A and the nearest leadwork pair * make a whole stitch, twist both pairs three times, set pin E between them and enclose the pin with a whole stitch and three twists *. Repeat from * to * across the row with each two pairs (pins F, G, H, I etc.). In the next row work the two pairs from F through the two pairs from G in whole stitch. Twist each pair three times. Repeat with pairs from H and I. These two rows are repeated until the space is filled.

Filling 29   Leadwork Bars

(Refer to diagram 187 and pattern 1: Shell.) Sew a pair into the braid at pinholes A and B. Make a whole stitch and twist each pair three times. Put a pin into the single pinhole 1. Work a leadwork towards pinhole C. Twist the pairs three times. Set a pin in hole 2, make a whole stitch, and twist each pair three times on the pin. Sew the outer pair into pinhole C, tie once, make a whole stitch, twist three times and put a pin into hole 3. Make the leadwork from hole 3 to hole 4 and repeat from 4 to 5 as from 2 to 3, until the last pinhole is reached. At the last pinhole, twist each pair three times and put a pin in the single pinhole; make a whole stitch, twist each pair three times and sew out each pair into the nearest two holes of the braid.

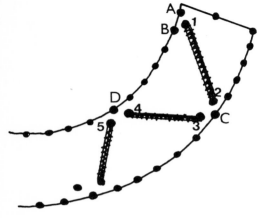

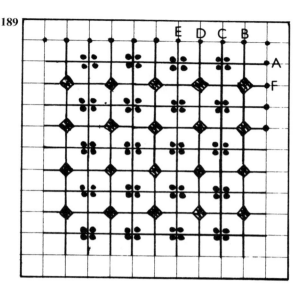

Filling 30   Swing Leadworks

(Refer to diagram 188 and pattern 17: Mat Sampler.) Sew one pair at holes A and B and tie each pair once. Twist each pair three times – (depending upon the size of the space to be filled, more twists may be necessary so that the single leadwork will lie in the central position). Work a small square leadwork. Twist the pairs three times and sew out at C and D, taking care not to pull the weaver thread. Tie each pair three times. These Swing Leadworks are only suitable to fill small spaces.

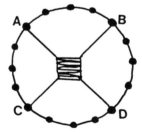

Filling 31   Blossom Variation

(Refer to diagram 189 and pattern 16: Sampler 3.) The pricking is the same as for Blossom filling *(filling 8)*, and the four holes are worked as instructed in filling 8. Sew two pairs at A, C and E for the blossom. Sew one pair at B, D, and F to work the row after the blossom and between each blossom. Twist the pair from B five times and use

the two pairs from A to work three half stitches of the plait. These two pairs then work through the single pair from B in whole stitch. Work three more half stitches to complete the plait between the blossom holes. Continue along this row working the blossom and through the single pair from E as above. The row will end with a plait and be sewn out. Return and work from right to left for each row. Twist the pairs from F and B five times; use these two pairs to make a leadwork (twist each pair five times after the leadwork has been made). Leave the pair on the right and use the left of the two pairs, which should contain the runner, to work in whole stitch through the two pairs of the blossom above. These two pairs should have three half stitches of the plait made before working through and three more will be made after working through to reach the four holes of the blossom below. Continue this row, working a leadwork with the pair from D (five twists before and after the leadwork) alternating with whole stitch through two pairs of the blossom and a leadwork made with the single pair between each blossom.

Filling 32   Cushion

(Refer to diagram 190 and pattern 16: Sampler 3.) This filling consists of rows of leadworks and pinholes. Sew two pairs at each of the top pinholes A, B, C and D. With each two pairs make a whole stitch and one twist, enclose the pin with a whole stitch and one twist. Take the right pair from A and the left pair from B to make a leadwork down to the next row of holes and leave. Next, make a leadwork with the right pair from B and the left from C. With one pair from B and the left from C make a whole stitch and twist once; put a pin in the hole below B, enclose with a whole stitch and one twist, then leave. Make a leadwork with the pairs from C and D. Continue likewise to the end of the row. If there is no space for a leadwork here, the odd pair will be sewn out; otherwise one extra pair will need to be sewn into the braid to work out this last leadwork.

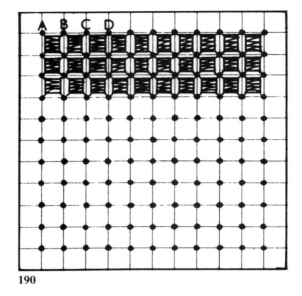

190

8

Leaves

Leaf 1   Divided Leaf

(Refer to Leaf Sampler: photograph 115, pricking 116 and diagram 117.) Begin at the bottom of the leaf and work the braid in the usual way, using the edge holes on the outside and the vein holes on the inside, and reduce the number of pairs as the work narrows near the top of the leaf. It will be necessary to back stitch in the last two or three holes on the vein side and the top vein hole should always be a back stitch which is not made up (i.e. the edge stitch not worked) until the top of the leaf has been turned. From here the runners work to the top outer hole of the leaf and make the edge stitch. Take the runners back through the coarse pair and tie them once before going on. Turn the pillow.

The procedure now varies according to whether any outside holes have to be worked to bring the work level with the top vein hole. If no outer holes need to be worked, take the tied runners through all the downrights and make up the back stitch in the top vein hole. If one outer hole has to be worked, take the tied runners through all downrights except the coarse pair, * leave the runners and use the last pair worked through as new runners to work to the outer edge and make the edge stitch. On return, work through all downrights and make up the back stitch in the top vein hole. * If two outer holes have to be worked, take the tied runners to within one pair of the coarse pair, leave the runners and use the last pair they worked through as new runners to work to the outer edge and make up the edge stitch. On return, work

through all downrights except the coarse pair and repeat from * to *.

Having made up the back stitch in the top vein hole, take the runners back to the outer edge, make the edge stitch and leave. Untwist the edge pair on the inner side and slip the coarse thread through (over and under) this pair – no edge pair will now be needed on this side. The coarse thread will hang next to the sewing. The second half of the leaf is usually worked in half stitch from here. Take the runners from the outside edge through all downrights (no twist at the end of the row) and sew them into the vein hole below the top one. Replace the pin after sewing, work to the outer edge with the sewn runners, make the edge stitch and leave.

Remove the pin from the top vein hole and pull the inner coarse thread *gently*. This has the effect of flattening the work round the top vein hole where the threads tend to bunch. Continue the braid, making edge holes on the outer side and sewing into the vein holes on the inner side. In lieu of back stitches on the inner side, sew twice in the same hole where necessary.

Leaf 2   Centre Leadwork and Pin

(Refer to Leaf Sampler: photograph 115, pricking 116 and diagram 117.) Set up at the top of the leaf with six pairs and a coarse pair and work three rows in whole stitch, then add one pair at each hole (14 pairs), then divide. Leave the runners at the outside edge and divide the pairs so that there are seven on each side. Take the four centre bobbins (one pair from each side) and make a whole stitch with them. Work the runners from the edge through to the middle and through the nearest of the two centre pairs. Twist the runners seven times and set a pin under them into the top hole of the division. Work back with these runners to the same edge and work an edge stitch there. Work back to the middle again, twist the runners seven times, set a pin under them in the next hole and leave them.

Take the remaining centre pair and use as runners to work to the other side, where the usual edge is made, then work back to the middle, twist seven times and set a pin under them. Each runner pair now works back to the edge on its own side and returns to the middle again; twist the runners three times, set a pin under each and use them to make a leadwork. Again, twist these pairs three times and work each runner pair out to its edge again. Continue the leaf, alternating pinholes and leadworks in the middle. The vein may be closed as for the ladder trail *(Leaf 7)*, but in the sampler two halves are sewn out separately.

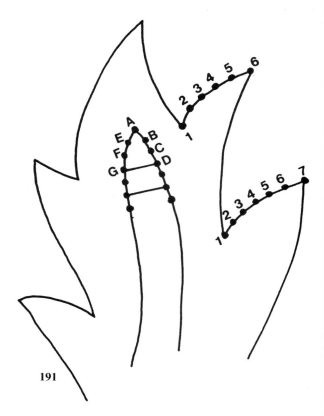

191

Leaf 3 Rib, Leadwork Centre and Points

(Refer to diagram 191 and Leaf Sampler: photograph 115, pricking 116 and diagram 117.) Start the rib which forms each side of the central vein by hanging ten pairs round a pin in hole A. Twist all pairs twice. Work a whole stitch with the two outer pairs on the left side and twist both pairs three times. The inner pair of these works through all but the last pair on the right side. Set pin B under the runners and work the normal edge stitch with the last pair. Now divide the bobbins into two halves with five pairs in each half. Take the innermost pair from each half and work a whole stitch with these. Work the runners through to the middle including the nearest pair from the central whole stitch. Twist the runners once and leave them. Work back with the last pair the runners passed through and make the next hole of the rib at C. Work one more row of rib, working to hole D.

The rib on the other side is begun by taking the remaining pair of the centre whole stitch as runners to E and making an edge stitch there. Work two more rows of rib on this side using holes F and G. From D and G bring the runner pair of each side through to the middle and use these to make a shallow leadwork (twist each pair once before and after the leadwork). Work each runner back to its own pinhole side and continue ribs making a leadwork after each second pin. Work the stem in whole stitch and finish as in Note 24.

Set up again at the outer tip of the leaf with six pairs; a coarse pair may be used. Work down to the point of centre rib in whole stitch, adding pairs on both sides. When the work is level with the top of the vein, the pairs are divided. Work the runners to the middle and sew them *(note 20f)* into hole A. Sew the next pair of downrights into the same hole, tie it once and use it as the runner pair for the other side. Each side is now worked independently, making edge holes on the outer sides and taking top sewings on the vein side. Work the right side first. The rows of

112

weaving must be kept level so that when the hole at the base of the first point is reached, the sewings in the vein side have not dropped below this level (in this case hole B, which will be used twice, once before the point is started and again when it is finished).

When pin 1 has been set, hang in two new pairs, laying these inside the coarse thread, and make up the edge stitch. Work through the coarse pair and one more pair, leave the runners and use the last pair they passed through to work to hole 2. Before making up the edge stitch here, hang in two new pairs which are laid inside the coarse thread and one pair which is laid to the back of the pillow.

* Make up the edge stitch, work back through the coarse pair, tie the runners once and work them through one more pair. Leave the runners and use the last pair they worked through as new runners to work to 3. Two more pairs are added here and laid inside the coarse thread. Repeat from * for holes 4 and 5. After making the edge stitch at 5, work through the coarse pair and tie the runners once, then take the tied runners through seven pairs to hole 2. Leave the runners and tie the last pair they passed through once. Use this pair as new runners to work to 6. Make the edge here. Bring the pair which was laid to the back of the pillow to the front and lay it to the left of the old runner pair left at 2. This fills in the tiny gap caused by the turn here in the last row. Tie the runners after they have passed through the coarse pair and then take them through all pairs to the centre vein, where they are sewn to hole B. Continue working the leaf taking out a pair at the next and several subsequent holes as the point narrows.

The method of working the point varies from the above description according to the shape of the point. For instance, the next point on this side is much sharper than the first. In this case, two pairs were hung in at 1 and 2, three pairs were hung in at 3, one of these being laid to the back of the pillow, and three more at 4, again putting one of these back. One pair was added at 5 and one at 6. From the point of 7 work back through five pairs to hole 4, tie the last pair passed through, leave the runners and use the tied pair to work to

the outer edge. Here the pair next to the coarse thread is taken out, and before working back to hole 3 bring in the pair laid back at 4. Work out to the edge again, take a pair out, bring in the pair laid back at 3 and then work back through all pairs to the rib in the middle. The other points are worked in a similar manner; most of the points will have fewer holes so these are worked accordingly. The other side is begun with the pair sewn in at A and worked in the same way. Half stitch may also be used for this leaf.

Leaf 4   Simple Raised Leaf

(Refer to Leaf Sampler: photograph 115, pricking 116, diagram 117.) Sew seven pairs into the stem at the base of the leaf and work a rib up the outer edge of the leaf. After setting the third pin from the tip of the leaf, and before making up the edge stitch, add a new pair. Bring this pair up around the pin as usual but do not lay it into the rib; lay it to the back of the pillow. Make the edge stitch, add another new pair at the next pin, laying it beside the first. After making the edge stitch and before working the next row of rib, take the first downright pair past the pin and lay it beside the other two pairs at the back (keep these pairs in the order in which they were laid aside). Work the last row of rib and set the pin in the top hole of the leaf. Turn the pillow after working the edge stitch.

Work the runners through the first downright pair and tie them once to keep this pair well up against the pin at the point. Continue with the tied runners through all the downright pairs, through the pair which was laid back and through the second of the new pairs which were added. Before taking the runners through this pair, tie it once to prevent it from slipping. This should be done with all laid in pairs before they are worked. Leave the runners and tie the last pair they passed through once. Use this tied pair as new runners to work to the outer edge and make the edge stitch. Work to the rib side again through all pairs, including the first new pair which was laid in. Leave the runners and tie the last pair through which they passed once. Use this tied pair as new runners to work towards the outer edge through three pairs. Twist the runner once to open the vein in the centre of the row and continue to the edge, where a new pair is added.

From now on, top sewings must be made whenever the runners reach the rib side, the first of these being made in the fourth hole from the top. This leaf in the sampler has been worked with a ladder trail centre, instructions as for Leaf 7. It could have a twisted vein or be completed in whole or half stitch.

When trying to decide where and when to begin adding new pairs to lay aside for filling in later, imagine that you are starting the leaf in the normal way from the tip and adding new pairs as the leaf widens. On one side, these are the positions where new pairs are laid in on the rib. Any new pairs needed on the other side will be added when working down the leaf later. This applies not only to leaves but to any raised, shaped section, such as petals, etc.

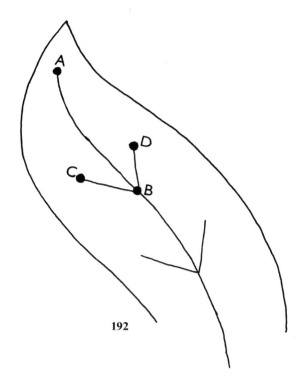

192

Leaf 5   Leaf with Raised Veins

(Refer to diagram 192 and Leaf Sampler: photograph 115, pricking 116 and diagram 117.) The raised vein is worked first and the half stitch leaf is worked afterwards in two parts. Begin at the top of the vein with seven pairs at A and work a rib with the pinholes on the left-hand side, finishing at pin B, where two pairs are hung in and placed inside the first downright thread, before the edge stitch is made. To work the first side vein lay the edge pairs of the rib aside *under* the first four downright pairs and use these four pairs to work a rib to top hole C, with the pinholes facing the base of the leaf. After the edge stitch at C, take leaders through to the plain side of the rib, tie them twice, lay all three pairs of the rib between them and tie them twice again over the pairs.

These pairs are now rolled down to B on the pinhole side. One pair can be left behind to attach the roll *(note 20g)*, or the roll can be sewn as it is being made, with the rolling pair, to each pinhole in turn. Do not sew at B. Lift the four pairs of the branch just made and lay them between the two bobbins of the nearest downright pair (not the edge pair which was laid aside, after edge stitch B

was made). Tie this downright pair twice over the four pairs of the side vein. Make another rib to D, using the first four pairs on this side (pinholes facing the base of the leaf). Tie and roll back as before, lay these pairs between the bobbins of the nearest downright pair and tie it over them twice. Tie three times any two pairs except the edge pair of the rib and cut off; continue the main rib to where the next side veins are to be made.

If the side veins do not come exactly opposite each other, they are worked as described above, but there is no need to hang in any extra pairs. The rib is sewn out at the base. Set up again at the top of the leaf, add a coarse pair here and work in half stitch to where the vein starts. Divide the downright pairs allowing more pairs to work the wider side. Work the runners to A and sew the runner – the leading thread of the last half stitch – to A *(note 20f)* and when the loop has been drawn through, put the *same* bobbins, i.e. the runner through the loop, tightening the loop carefully and easing it down with the needlepin, so that it does not lock on the thread until it has reached the pinhole. This type of sewing also applies when the backing is made in whole stitch. Sew the next downright pair into the same hole and use it as a runner for the other side of the leaf. Both sides are now worked independently, making pinholes on the outer side and top sewings on the vein side. When the tops of the side veins are reached the runner is sewn into them (as described for A) before continuing the row. Work well down and level with this hole before making the sewing to avoid a gap forming in the half stitch. The side veins in this pattern are so short that the sewing at the top of the vein is sufficient. Where a longer rib is backed with half stitch (or whole stitch) it will be necessary to sew the runners once or twice in holes in other parts of the vein.

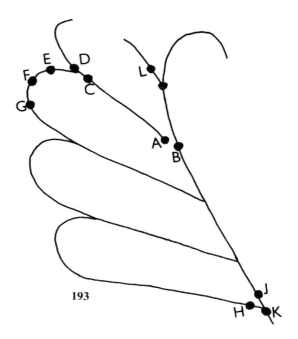

193

Leaf 6   Raised Leaf with Taps

(Refer to diagram 193 and Leaf Sampler: photograph 115, pricking 116 and diagram 117.) The little sections in this leaf are called 'taps' in Honiton lace. Work the rib forming the centre vein first, sewing in seven pairs and working with the pinholes on the left of the rib. Work the rib right up to the point of the highest central tap. At the third hole from the top, hang in a new pair, bringing it round the pin as usual, but then laying it to the back of the pillow. Make up the edge. Hang in another pair at the next hole, laying it aside with the other new pair. Before working back take the first downright pair past the pin and lay it back next to the other two laid in pairs. The next pin is the topmost one, and after making the edge, turn the pillow.

Work through the first downright pair and tie the runners once. Work the tied runners through all the other downright pairs including the pair which was laid back from the rib and the second of the pairs which were laid in. Leave the runners. Tie the last pair the runners passed through once, and use this pair as new runners to work to the edge. When returning to the rib side, work through all pairs, including the first new pair which was laid in. Leave the runners, tie this pair and use it as new runners to work to the edge.

From now on the runners are top sewn into the rib holes, the first sewing being made into the hole below the one at which the pair was laid in (the fourth hole from the top). Work to the bottom of the tap and take out one pair near the bottom. After the last hole A on the pinhole side, work the runners through to B and sew them there. This last sewing into the rib should always be just below the level of the last hole on the pinhole side.

Tie the sewn runners twice. Put one of the downright pairs on the left aside; open the sewn pair, lift all the other bobbins and lay them down in between the bobbins of the sewn pair. Tie the sewn pair over the bunch twice. Lay aside another pair out of the bunch on the left. Take the bobbins of the bunch in one hand and the tied pair in the other and wind this tied pair round and round the bunched bobbins to make a neat firm roll which should reach up to C. Sew the pair which has done the winding in at D. This is not a top sewing. Insert the needlepin in hole D and bring the point out under the bunch. Draw one of the threads of the winding pair through and put the other through the loop over the bunch. This fastens the roll to the hole.

Tie the sewn pair twice, twist it three times and

leave aside to become the edge pair for the next tap. Take the pair which was left out of the bunch and use it to stitch the roll along the side of the first completed tap, by sewing over the roll into each hole after A, as described for the sewing at D. Tie the pair once after each sewing. After sewing into hole C, tie the sewn pair twice and use it as the runner pair to work through the pairs of the roll to the outer side (first having straightened these a little). Twist the runners three times, set pin E under them and hang in a new pair, bringing this round the pin and laying it aside, to be used when filling in the clothwork later. Work the edge stitch with the pair from D. Work a rib across the top of the second tap. * Hang in and lay aside one pair at F, also lay back the pair of downrights nearest the pin before working the next row of rib. Repeat from * at G.

After setting pin G and making the edge, work runners through all pairs, including the pairs that were laid aside, to E. Leave the runners and tie the last pair they worked through, using this pair as new runners. Continue working this tap, making top sewings into the edge of the first tap (over the roll). After the sewing at A, lay in the pair which was left here, to fill the little gap which may appear at this point. The remaining taps on this side are worked similarly.

At the end of each tap the pairs should be reduced to the number needed to make the roll and rib for the next tap and allowing for a pair to fill the gap at the base of the tap. When the last tap has been completed, the threads are rolled up and attached to the centre vein to begin the highest tap on the other side. In this case the rows of weaving are arranged in such a way so that after pin H has been set the runners work to J, where they are sewn and tied twice. The edge pair from H is sewn at K and also tied twice. Bunch the remaining bobbins, cross the sewn pairs under the bunch and tie them over the bunch. Leave one pair behind and make a roll to reach to L, where the rolling pair is sewn in. Use the pair left behind to attach the roll. The second row of taps is worked as the first.

Leaf 7 Ladder Trail (or Mittens)

(Refer to Leaf Sampler: photograph 115, pricking 116 and diagram 117.) This is often indicated on the pattern by a line of widely spaced holes down the centre of a whole stitch leaf. Work three rows, then divide the downrights in half (if there is an odd pair in the middle, add it to the side furthest from the runners). Work the runners through to the middle, twist them three times and leave them. Take the next pair of downrights and use them as runners to work to the other side. Make the edge stitch there and work back to the middle. Twist the runners three times. * Work a whole stitch with the two twisted runner pairs in the middle and twist both pairs three times. The left-hand pair works out to the left edge, the right-hand pair out to the right edge. Make the edge stitches on each side and work both sets of runners back to the middle. Twist both runner pairs three times and repeat from *.

When three or four pinholes of leaf remain, close the ladder trail by working both sets of runners to the middle. Decide which edge hole is to be worked next. If it is a hole on the left, drop the left of the two runner pairs in the middle, and with the right runner pair work through it and onto the left side. If the next edge hole to be worked is on the right, reverse the above, dropping the right pair and work through with the left. The dropped runners become downrights. Continue the braid. The ladder trail tends to become too wide, unless care is taken to pull the downrights on both sides towards the middle after every row.

9
Notes on Techniques

Note 1 Starting Honiton braid at a point

(Refer to diagram 194.) This occurs when starting leaves, stems, etc.

(a) Whole stitch

Wind knots connecting the pairs a little way back onto one of the bobbins. Hang six pairs round a pin in hole A, so that the knotted threads are in the middle – i.e. the first four bobbins on the left are knot-free and so are the first two bobbins on the right. These are the runners and the two edge pairs. (If B is on the left of A, instead of as shown here, the four knot-free bobbins should be on the outside right and the two on the outside left.) Twist all pairs twice. Take the pair wound with coarse thread, one bobbin in each hand, slip the thread under all central bobbins, omitting the knot-free pairs at the sides, and lay the coarse bobbins to the back of the pillow. Work a whole stitch with the outside pairs on the left, twist both pairs three times and take the inner of these two pairs as runners through all pairs except the last.

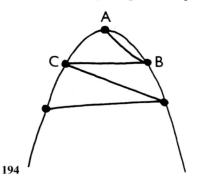

194

Twist the runners three times and set pin B under them. Work a whole stitch with the runners and the edge pair and twist both pairs three times. Bring the coarse threads down into position, to lie third from the left and fifth from the right, making sure that this thread lies inside pin B *.

The coarse thread is treated as a downright and makes a pair with the thread lying inside it. This pair is called the 'coarse pair' and the runners are always worked through it in whole stitch. Continue the braid, using the second pair from the right as runners and working them through all pairs except the last on the left. Twist the runners three times and set pin C under them. Work a whole stitch with the runners and edge pair and twist both pairs three times.

If the space between B and C is a wide one, or if quite a number of new pairs have to be added soon, start with eight pairs round pin A.

(b) Half stitch

Wind the knots further back onto the bobbins, as knots in half stitch are awkward to deal with. Begin exactly as above, working in whole stitch as far as *. Using the inner pair of the two which made the edge stitch at B as runners, ** work a whole stitch through the coarse pair, twist runners once and continue in half stitch through all downright pairs until the coarse pair on the other side is reached. Work a whole stitch through this pair, twist runners three times, set pin C under them and work a whole stitch with the runners and edge pair. Twist both pairs three times.

117

Using the inner of these two pairs as runners, continue from **.

Note 2 Hanging in new pairs

Always hang in new pairs on the outside of the curve.

(a) In whole stitch braid
After setting the pin and before working the edge stitch, take the new pair, one bobbin in each hand, and slip the thread under the runners. Take both bobbins of the new pair in one hand and slide the thread up the runners and round the pin just set, from the outside in. Lay the new pair inside the coarse thread, or, if no coarse thread is being used, inside the first downright thread, with the knot-free bobbin next to the coarse thread. Complete the edge stitch.

(b) In half stitch braid
Proceed as above but, having laid the new pair inside the coarse thread, twist the inner bobbin of the new pair with the next bobbin on the inside. Complete the edge stitch.

(c) Inside a purl edge
Take the runners to the purl edge. When they have passed through the coarse pair, twist them three times, slip the new pair under them and lay it to the back of the pillow. Complete the purl (note 9) and, before working the runners back through the coarse pair, bring the new pair from the back of the pillow and lay it inside the coarse thread (twist the inner bobbin of the new pair with the next bobbin on the inside if working in half stitch).

(d) Hanging in two pairs
Normally only one pair is hung in at a time but occasionally, if the space to be filled widens very suddenly, it may be necessary to hang in two pairs at the same pinhole. These may both be hung in as described above, but the following method is also used. Add the first pair in the usual way, make up the edge stitch and twists and then hang the second pair round the runners (second pair from the edge). Lay this new pair to the back of the pillow and work the runners through to the other side. Before returning, take the new pair from the back of the pillow and lay it inside the coarse thread.

(e) Adding extra pairs
When it is necessary to add extra pairs on the sewing side of the work, they should be sewn into the lower loop of the previous pinhole, laid into position inside the coarse thread if one is being used, or inside the first thread, and worked before the next sewing is taken.

Note 3 Taking out pairs

Always take out pairs on the inside of a curve.

(a) In whole stitch braid
When the braid narrows and the clothwork becomes too thick, unwanted pairs are simply cut off. Normally the two downrights next to the coarse thread are taken out, but if any downrights have knots coming close to the lace, these should be cut off first. Although two threads must be cut off at a time, these need not necessarily be adjacent; as the clothwork is thick, any irregularity in the weaving will not be noticeable.

(b) In half stitch braid
Work towards the side on which a pair is to be taken out until only three pairs remain unworked (i.e. the edge pair, the coarse pair and the pair next to this). Work in *whole stitch* through the next two pairs, before working the usual edge stitch. Take the two bobbins inside the coarse thread (i.e. the two middle bobbins of the two whole stitches), tie them three times close to the lace, but not so close that they will force the weaving up, and cut them off. This can be done at either or both ends of the row, wherever it is most convenient or the shape of the braid demands it, provided a whole stitch is worked with the pair inside the coarse thread above the two bobbins to be taken out.

Note 4   Back stitch

The rows of whole stitch or half stitch should always be at right angles to the lines of pinholes and the work should not be allowed to slope. If it does, a hole on one side must be used more than once, in order to give the other side a chance to catch up. This is done with a back stitch. Work towards the side on which a pinhole is to be used twice. After passing through the coarse pair, twist the runners once and set the pin under them. Do not work the stitch with the edge pair but weave the runners back to the other side and make the usual edge there. Weave runners to the back stitch side and twist them three times after passing through the coarse pair. Remove the pin and replace it into the same hole but under the runners and not into the little loop that it was holding before (this loop tends to disappear as the work progresses). Work the usual edge stitch and three twists (this is called 'making up the back stitch').

When working around a very tight bend, continual back stitching would make the braid too thick and lumpy on the inner edge. In this case, alternate back stitches with working the runners to within the coarse pair on the inner side, leaving them there and working back to the outer edge with the last pair of downrights the runners pass through.

Note 5   Preventing braid pulling away from the pins

This tends to happen on the outer side of a sharp curve or corner, resulting in elongated, unsightly pinholes, and can be avoided as follows. Having worked the pinhole at the apex of the curve or corner, take the runners back through the coarse pair and tie them once. Continue with the tied runners to the other side of the braid. The knot keeps the coarse pair up against the pin.

Note 6   Weaver's knot

(Refer to diagram 195.) This knot is used for joining short broken threads. Make a slip loop in the end of the thread on the bobbin. Pull the other broken end through this loop until the loop

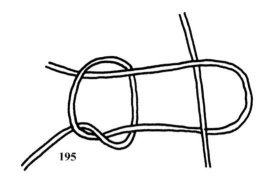

195

is where you want the knot to be. Take hold of the ends of the slip loop, one in each hand, and pull them apart until the loop has disappeared and the other thread has been pulled into the knot. Test the knot by pulling on the bobbin; if the knot slips off the end of the broken thread, it has not been tied properly – try again.

Note 7   Getting rid of knots

(a) In whole stitch braid
Simply loop the knotted thread round a pin higher up in the lace so that the knot is in the loop and lay the bobbin back in its position and continue the braid. The loop with the knot in it can be trimmed off later when there is no danger of the thread being pulled out.

(b) In half stitch braid
It is best to avoid knots in half stitch braid, but occasionally a thread does break and a knot has to be coped with. If the thread has broken close to the lace, it is necessary to undo the lace until the end can be tied to the thread on the bobbin, using a weaver's knot *(note 6)*. Continue to undo the lace until the knotted thread is near enough to the end of the row to be taken out in the normal way *(note 3b)*. A new pair will have to be hung in to compensate for the removed pair, unless the braid is becoming narrower. The knot may be further down the thread, where it would become worked into the lace if the thread were allowed to continue in half stitch but where, if the thread were allowed to hang straight down, it would be sewn out or tied out before the knot is reached. In this case, continue working the braid

until the knotted thread can be exchanged with the partner of the coarse thread (the coarse pair being the only threads in half stitch which hang straight down).

(c) In a long braid

Should a knot appear in the coarse thread when working a long braid, lay the knotted thread on a pin to the back of the pillow and bring back into position again. The loop can be cut off when the work has been completed.

Note 8   Leadworks (tallies, woven plaits, cutworks)

(Refer to diagram 196.) These are much used in Honiton fillings and are always either square or oblong in shape and never have pointed ends, as is the case in some other laces. Two pairs are required, usually twisted several times, according

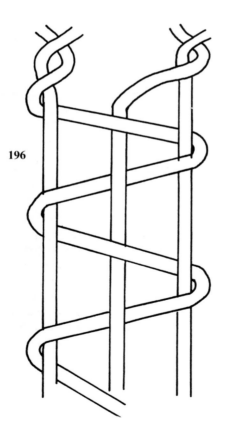

196

to the filling being worked. Lengthen the second thread from the left and use it as a weaver to weave over the third thread, under and back over the fourth, under the third, over and back under the first. Repeat this sequence of weaving once more, then pull up by gently pulling the weaver whilst holding down the other three bobbins and keeping them slightly spread. Alternate rows of weaving and pulling up until the leadwork is the desired length. The weaver must not be allowed to drop, otherwise the leadwork will be drawn up out of shape. The leadwork can be made wide or narrow, depending on how far apart the outer bobbins are held. The pairs are then twisted again.

Note 9   Purls

Work towards the purl edge, through the coarse pair and twist the runners three times. Work a whole stitch with the runners and edge pair. Twist the outside pair seven times. Take a pin and, holding it with the point towards the braid, place it under the outer thread of the twisted pair. Twist the pin over the thread, towards you and down, and set it into the hole. Twist the second bobbin of the pair round the pin from the outside in, and lay it down inside the outer bobbin. Twist the pair once if the purl is being made on the right-hand side of a braid; for a purl on the left-hand side, the pair is crossed twice, left over right. Work a whole stitch with the edge pair, twist both pairs three times and take the inner pair as runners back into the lace.

Note 10   Sewing forgotten purls onto an edge

Sew one pair into the hole in the braid previous to the hole in which the purl is needed. Twist seven times, make a purl (note 9), setting the pin under the braid, into the pinhole in the pricking where the purl is required (take the second bobbin of the pair round the pin from the outside in, and twist once as usual). Sew into the same braid hole and tie once. * Twist seven times to make the next purl, using the next hole in the pricking and at the end sewing into the braid hole. Tie once. Continue from * until all missing purls have been added. Tie three times at the end and cut off.

Note 11 Four pin bud

(Refer to diagram 197.) In whole stitch braid, work until level with top hole 1 and leave runners at edge. Divide downrights in half; if there is an odd pair in the middle, add it to the half nearest the runners. Take runners through to the middle and two pairs more. With the last pair the runners passed through, work back through two pairs. Twist the two middle pairs of these four three times, set pin in hole 1 between them and enclose pin with a whole stitch, twist both pairs three times.

Use the two outer pairs of the four middle pairs as runners and take each to its respective edge; make the edge stitches (or, more likely, a back stitch) and work back to the middle, leaving the twisted middle pairs unworked. Twist each runner pair three times and set pins 2 and 3 under them. With each runner pair and the nearest of the two twisted middle pairs work a whole stitch and twist all four pairs three times. Again use the two outer pairs of the four middle pairs as runners to work to the edges; make edge stitches (or back stitches) and work back again to the middle, leaving the two twisted middle pairs

197

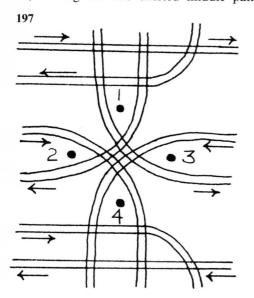

unworked. With these two twisted middle pairs work a whole stitch, twist both pairs three times and set pin in hole 4 between them. Do not enclose this pin.

Decide which edge hole is to be worked next; if it is at the right edge, take the right-hand runners through the remaining three middle pairs to the left. If the next hole to be worked is at the left edge, take the left-hand runners through the remaining three middle pairs to the right. Leave the runners, and use the last pair they worked through as runners to work to the edge at which the next hole is to be worked; make the edge stitch, and continue the braid. The other runners stay where they are and become downrights.

Note 12 Windows

Worked in whole stitch braid. This is a line of small holes across the entire width of a whole stitch braid, sometimes used as a vein in a leaf or flower. The braid should be fairly open, with not too many downrights in it, otherwise the windows will not show up well. Work the runners through the coarse pair, twist them three times and * work a whole stitch with the next pair. Twist both pairs three times. Continue from * until runners arrive at the coarse pair, on the other side. This should not be twisted. Finish the row as usual. In the next row, only the runner pair is twisted three times after each stitch. The downrights are not twisted.

Note 13 Small hole in whole stitch braid

Work the runners to where the hole is needed. Twist the runners and the last pair they passed through three times. Work a whole stitch with the next downright pair and twist this three times, but do not twist the runners. Work runners on to the edge. In the next row, the runners only are twisted three times, immediately below the three twists made by the runners in the last row. Continue the braid.

Note 14   Snatch-pin hole with leadwork in whole stitch braid

(Refer to diagram 198.) This usually consists of eight or ten pinholes pricked in a circle. Work until level with the top snatch-pin hole and leave runners at the edge. Divide downrights in half; if there is an odd pair in the middle, add it to the half nearest the runners. Work the runners through to the middle and one pair more and leave. With the last pair which the runners passed through, work back through two pairs. With the two middle pairs of these four make a whole stitch, twist each pair three times, set pin A between them and enclose the pin with a whole stitch but do not twist. Using these two pairs as runners, work the left pair out to the left edge and the right pair out to the right edge, make up the edge stitches and work back to the middle. Twist both runner pairs seven times and set pins under them into holes B and C. Work out to the edges (back stitching if necessary) and back again to the middle, leaving the last downright pair on each side unworked (to be used for the leadwork later). Twist the runners seven times and set pins under them on each side. The runners continue to work out to the edges and back to the middle, twisting seven times round the snatch pins and back stitching, if necessary, on the outer edges to keep the work level.

No hole on the outer edges should be worked below the level of the snatch-pin hole, otherwise gaps will appear around the hole on each side. Continue until only the last three holes of the snatch-pin hole are unworked and leave. Twist each of the pairs left hanging from pins B and C three or four times, depending on the size of the hole, make a small, square leadwork with them and twist them three or four times again. Work the runners through these two pairs before

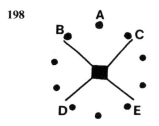

198

twisting and setting pins D and E under them. Work both runners to the edges again and back to the centre, twist one runner pair seven times and set a pin under it into the last hole, but do not enclose the pin. Take the other runners through this pair (which now become downrights) to the other edge. Continue the normal braid.

Note 15   Crossing the coarse threads

(Refer to diagram 199.) A pinhole in the middle of the braid often denotes that the coarse threads are to be crossed. This is done to make a division in the braid, or to separate areas of whole stitch and half stitch. Work the braid until the holes on both sides of the central hole have been made up. When one side of the braid is straight and the other curved, arrange the stitches so that the leaders can be left on the curved side.

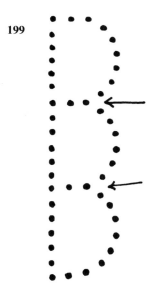

199

Lengthen the coarse thread on the curved side and weave it through the downrights, round the coarse thread on the other side and back through the downrights to its original position. It is always best to begin the weaving by taking the coarse thread over its neighbour and under the next thread. Pull up the weaving thread by pulling it against the other coarse thread, which should be held taut in the other hand. Shorten the coarse thread again and continue the braid, tying the runners once after they have passed through the coarse pair, to keep this up in position.

Note 16   Crossing one braid over another

Work the braid to where it has to cross an already completed part. After making up the last hole, work one more row. Sew the runners and edge pairs into appropriate holes of the completed braid, tying them three times. Bunch the bobbins, cross the two sewn edge pairs under the bunch and tie them three times over the bunch. The tied edge pairs and one other pair are then sewn into appropriate holes on the other side of the completed braid, the bobbins are more or less disentangled, and the braid is continued in the usual way.

Note 17   Dividing a braid into two

Work until level with the top hole of the division, and leave the runners at one edge. Do not work any edge holes below the level of this top hole – if necessary leave a back stitch at one edge to avoid this. Sort out the two middle pairs of downrights, pushing the other bobbins a little way away on each side. Take one of the outer bobbins of the two middle pairs and lay it with the bobbins of the nearest side section. Take the innermost bobbin of the other side section and lay it with the three bobbins remaining in the middle. There are now two pairs in the middle and an odd number of bobbins in each side section. Take a new pair wound with coarse thread and weave the thread through the two middle pairs. Lay this pair to the back of the pillow.

With the two middle pairs work a whole stitch and twist both pairs three times. Work the runners from the edge through the bobbins of the nearest side section, bringing down the nearest coarse thread from the back of the pillow to join the odd bobbin at the end of the section. Work the runners through this pair, twist them three times and set a pin under them into the top hole of the division. Hang a new pair round the runners, laying it to the back of the pillow (this

will be needed later as runner pair for the other branch); make a whole stitch with the runners and the nearest twisted middle pair. Twist both pairs three times.

Continue this branch of the braid, bring down the other coarse thread from the back of the pillow to lie in between the other side section and the remaining twisted middle pair. If the second branch is not to be worked for some time, it is advisable to lengthen these threads so that the bobbins hang over the side of the pillow, with one of the cover cloths pinned over them. Be careful when handling the pillow not to snap these bobbins off.

When returning to the second branch of the braid, bring down the pair which was hung in earlier and work it as runner pair to the outer edge. Work back to the inner side, using the remaining twisted middle pair as edge pair.

Note 18   Rib (ten-stick, stem stitch)

This has pinholes on one side only and can be made with any number of pairs from four to about eight pairs. If the line of holes is curved, work the rib with the pinholes on the outer side of the curve. Set a pin in the first hole and hang the pairs round it, twist all pairs twice, or sew the required number of pairs into an already completed part of the work (in which case do not twist). Work a whole stitch with the two outer pairs on the pinhole side and twist both pairs three times. * Work the inner of these two pairs to the plain side through all pairs. Twist the runners once and leave them. Work the last pair the runners passed through as new runners to the pinhole side through all pairs except the last. Twist the runners three times, set the pin in the next hole under them, make the usual edge stitch, and twist each pair three times. Repeat from *. After setting the last pin, work the runners to the plain side and sew out as usual.

An alternative method of making the plain edge is to work the runners from the pinhole side through all pairs to the plain side, then make a second stitch with the runners and the last pair they passed through. The inner pair of these two then works back to the pinhole side.

Note 19   Crossing one rib over another

Take the runners to the plain side, sew them into the nearest hole of the rib to be crossed, and tie them once. Sew the edge pair on the other side into the next or next but one hole (depending on the width of the rib being worked) of the rib being crossed, tie them once, and twist them three times. Continue the rib by taking the runners from the plain side through the passives and working the next pinhole.

Note 20   Sewings

(Refer to diagram 200.)

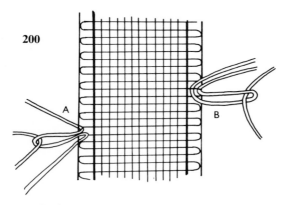

200

(a) Ordinary sewings

When the work in progress has to be joined into an already completed part, this is done by means of 'sewings'. These are made by drawing one of the pair of threads to be joined through an edge hole of the completed braid to form a loop, passing the other bobbin of the pair through this loop, and pulling up both threads. Remove the pin from the edge hole of the completed braid, to which the join is to be made. Insert a needlepin into this braid hole, and bring the point of the needlepin out under the edge of the braid. Press one of the threads of the pair to be joined under the needle point and manoeuvre this back into the hole in the pricking, taking a loop of the thread with it. Holding the bobbin so that this thread is quite taut, slowly draw the needlepin out of the hole, and at the same time bend the handle end down. At the last moment, slacken the thread, and flick the needle point out of the

hole and through the hole in the braid, and the loop of thread should come out with it. Pass the other bobbin through this loop and pull up. Replace the pin. It is important to make the sewing into the pinhole and not into the space between two pinholes. Sewings require some practice before they can be made easily.

(b) Top sewings or raised sewings

These are used mainly for raised work, or where a particularly close join is required, or when sewing out fillings, when the cut ends of threads are not so likely to show on the right side, as in an ordinary sewing. This sewing is made round one of the little side bars of the pinhole. Insert the needlepin into the pinhole to which the sewing is to be made, and bring the point of the needle out from under the side bar. Draw one of the pairs of threads through and complete as for an ordinary sewing.

(c) Sewing in new pairs into a completed braid

This is used for fillings, or to work another adjoining piece of braid. Insert the needlepin into the pinhole of the completed braid and bring the point out under the edge. Press the thread connecting the new pair under the needle point, take both bobbins of the new pair into one hand and lift them, so that the needlepin can be slid into the hole in the pricking with a loop of thread. Bring the loop of thread through and put one of the pair of bobbins through it. Pull up both bobbins. Replace the pin in the pinhole. When sewing in pairs for fillings, it is sometimes found that the pinholes are not placed in exactly the positions in which the pairs are wanted. In this case, after sewing into the nearest pinhole, the pair may be tied once, pulling it to the left or right of the pinhole (whichever is required), before tightening the knot.

(d) Sewing out pairs from a filling

The pairs are sewn into the completed braid as described above (20b), after which they are tied three times each and laid back to be cut off later, when all the pairs from the filling have been sewn out. If necessary, more than one pair can be sewn into the same hole in the braid.

124

When sewing out the pairs which have made a leadwork, sew out the pair which contains the weaver first, if this is possible, pulling the thread which is not the weaver through to make the loop, then passing the weaver through this loop carefully, and pull up. Then sew out the other pair.

(e) Sewings where two rows of pinholes meet

When the braid being worked approaches close to an already completed braid, the two should be joined, even though each has its own edge holes. When the pin has been set, and the edge stitch made, do not twist the pairs. Remove the pin from the hole in the adjacent braid in which the join is to be made, and sew the edge pair to it. Now work a whole stitch with the other runners, twist both pairs three times and continue working after replacing the pin.

(f) Sewing into a hole in which braid was started at a point

Since several loops hang round this pin, the pinhole would be lost if the pin were removed for the sewing. Therefore the sewing should be made with the pin in position. Insert the needlepin close by the pin and bring it out under the loops held by the pin. Complete the sewing in the usual way.

(g) Sewings to attach a roll to a completed edge

When a roll has been made in raised work, a pair is usually left out of the roll and used to attach the roll to each hole of a completed edge. Remove the pin from the first hole. Insert the needlepin into the hole, and bring it out under the completed edge and under the roll, and hook through one of the threads of the sewing pair. Complete the sewing in the usual way. Tie the sewing pair once and replace the pin. Repeat this process up the roll, and tie the sewing pair twice after the last sewing.

(h) Sewings made easy

(Refer to diagram 201.) When setting up pairs on a pin to start a section of lace, and where a sewing

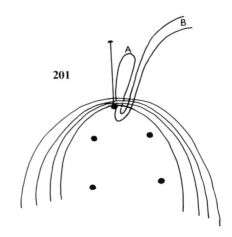

201

will be needed at this pinhole later, take a piece of thread (as used to make the lace) about 12 in. in length, double this to make a loop at one end A with two loose ends at B.

Lay the double thread under half of the threads at one side and put to the back of the pillow, they can be pinned down until ready to be used. This method can also be used in raised work, i.e. when the threads are turned to roll up to work the next section. The double thread should then be laid under the runner at the last pinhole where the turn is to be made. When the work reaches the pinhole where the sewing is to be made, put one bobbin of the pair to be sewn through the loop A and gently pull the two threads at B. The thread to be sewn will come through the pinhole and the second bobbin can be passed through the loop and the sewing made. The loose thread can then be gently pulled away to be used again at the next difficult sewing hole.

Note 21   Laying in pairs for subsequent use

When the part being worked passes the place where the next braid will later begin, it is possible to hang in the pairs which will be needed for the braid, and so save having to sew them in. They can be hung on the runners at the holes above the section to be worked later, both before and after the edge stitch has been made, and laid aside. This is not always practicable, and can only be decided by studying the pattern.

Note 22   Adding the coarse pair when not starting at a point

When starting a piece of braid for which the pairs are sewn in or laid in previously, the coarse pair must be woven through the downrights and placed to the back of the pillow, until the first row has been worked to keep it in place. An alternative way is to hang the coarse pair round a pin above the piece to be worked and lay it in position immediately. The ends of the coarse thread can be cut off when the section is completed.

Note 23   Sewing out a braid

(a) Sewing out a braid into a braid

When the last edge hole has been worked, take the runners back through all pairs except the runners on the other side. This final row is always worked in whole stitch, even when it follows half stitch braid. Lay back the coarse threads. The pairs are now sewn into an already completed part of the work. Two or even three pairs may be sewn into each hole of the completed braid. The runners and edge pairs should always be sewn and as many pairs as possible in between. Tie all sewn and unsewn pairs three times. Bunch the bobbins, cross the two sewn outer pairs under the bunch and tie them three times over the bunch – i.e. take one bobbin from each pair, tie them three times, then take the other bobbin from each pair and tie them. Cut off all pairs, using the method described in note 25. If the braid being sewn out is very wide, it is better to form two bunches, making sure that the pairs which are crossed under and tied over the bunches are sewn pairs. Trim off all the ends of thread and the coarse threads close to the lace, taking care not to cut into the knots.

(b) To sew out a braid or a rib into a rib

After the last pinhole and the final row have been worked, only the edge pairs and runners are sewn and tied – the downright pairs should be tied without sewing and the pairs are bunched and cut off in the normal way. If desired, one of the pairs which were thrown out before the sewing

out began, may be used to tie back the bunch of threads over the braid. No ends should be seen when the lace is turned over. With experience, it is possible to tie the sewn pairs so well back into the pinhole loop that when bunched and cut off the ends do not show.

When a rib is sewn out after the last pin is set, work to the plain side, then sew out and tie runners, the pair next to them and the edge pair on the pinhole side. Cut out two pairs of downrights from the centre of the rib, tie the remaining pairs, and bunch and tie as usual.

Note 24   Finishing a braid at a point

(Refer to diagram 202.) Cut out pairs as the braid narrows. Lay aside two pairs on one side near the end (inside the coarse thread at pins A and B in the diagram); these will be wanted again. After setting pin C and making the edge stitch, cut out the coarse threads and take the runners through all remaining pairs, including the edge pair on the other side (without twisting). Tie all pairs three times, beginning with the runners.

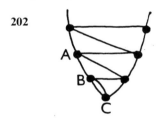

202

Bunch the bobbins, cross the outside pairs under the bunch and tie them three times over the bunch. Remove every alternate pin and push the remainder down into the pillow, leaving the last two or three on each side standing. The two pairs which were laid aside must now be spread out, so that one bobbin of each pair lies on each side of the lace. Turn all the bunched bobbins back over the lace between the standing pins and tie the spread pairs three times over the bunch. Cut off.

Note 25   Bowing off

Honiton bobbins are usually cut off from the pillow and tied together ready for the next piece of work in one action, using a pair of small, blunt scissors with points. Hold the pair to be cut off loosely in one hand and place the pair of scissors – points closed – under the pair of threads to be cut off. Twist the point of the scissors over the thread, towards you and down, so that a loop of thread forms round the scissors. Open the scissors and catch the thread running from the scissors to the lace between the blades from underneath. Close the scissors (if they are blunt enough they should not cut the threads) and move the bobbins towards the lace, still holding them so that the threads are quite slack, until the loop slides off the points of the scissors, a new loop is held in the blades and a knot is formed. Tighten the knot by pulling the thread between the bobbins and the top loop taut, open the scissors and cut the loop. Pull the bobbins away – they will be found to be tied. If there are knots in the threads to be cut off or on the bobbins, where they will soon work out, it is best to unwind the bobbins, so that the pairs can be bowed off below the knots, which are left behind on the threads to be trimmed off from the lace.

Note 26   Pinning down the completed lace

When a section is finished, or when the pins begin to get in the way of the part being worked, every other pin can be removed and the remainder pushed right down into the pillow. When doing this, while the work is still in progress, leave at least 1 cm ($\frac{1}{2}$ in.) of pins standing on each side of the part being worked.

Note 27   Starting a leaf with a purl at the top hole

(Refer to diagram 203.) Hang six pairs and the coarse pair, as usual at pin A, which in this case is the first hole at the side of the leaf. Work across

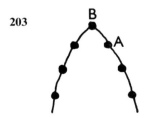

203

to the top hole (B) and make a purl. Tie back the coarse pair *(note 5)* and work to A again. Gently take out the pin, make the purl in A and tie the runners well back against the coarse pair again. Continue working as normal, adding new pairs.

Note 28   Rubbings

This is a convenient way of obtaining copies of prickings. Lay the pricking, wrong or rough side uppermost, on a table, place a piece of thin paper (copy paper, airmail writing paper, etc.) over it and, holding this down firmly, rub lightly over the pattern with a piece of heelball. This can be obtained from a shoe repair shop or from a shop selling artists' materials (as it is also used for brass rubbings). The pinholes from the pricking will be transferred onto the paper.

Note 29   Markings on patterns

Occasionally odd holes are found on Honiton prickings and it is useful to know their meaning. Two holes close together in the middle of a braid mean that this portion is to be worked in half stitch. Four holes, grouped as for a four pin bud and pricked on the card outside the pattern, indicate where purls should be made. This is often accompanied by a line scratched on the pattern outside the outer holes to another group of four holes, showing the extent of the purl edge. A single hole between the two edges of the braid shows where the coarse thread crosses, or may also indicate a hole (for an eye, nail, etc.). Which of these is intended can usually be seen by studying the pattern. A line of widely spaced holes indicates a twisted vein, ladder trail or windows.

Note 30   Working threads from one section to another

First method
(Refer to diagram 204a.) Work to 1 and make a back stitch at this hole. Work to 2 and sew the runner pair and the edge pairs at this hole. Tie the edge pair three times at this hole and lay aside to be cut off later. With the sewn runners work

through one pair. Tie the runners once and work them through two more pairs. * Leave the runners and with the last pair they work through, work back to hole 3. Sew the runners here. Take the two bobbins inside the coarse bobbin or, if a coarse thread is not being used, inside the first bobbin, tie them three times and cut them out. Work the sewn runners again through three pairs, and repeat from * twice (holes 4 and 5). From 5 the sewn runners are taken through all downrights to 1, to make up the back stitch there. Work to 6 and sew the runners there. Tie the runners once, twist them three times and leave them to become an edge pair. The threads are now in position to work the adjoining section. Take the edge pairs left at 1 as runners out to the outer edge and work the next pinhole there. Continue the next section taking sewings on the inner side.

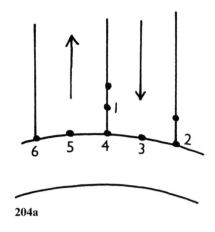

204a

Second method

(Refer to diagram 204b.) Sometimes the two sections are not joined as above. In this case, work as above until the runners have been sewn at 6. Work the sewn runners to 7 and make the edge stitch there. Before returning, sew a new pair at 6, twist it three times and use it as the new edge pair on this side.

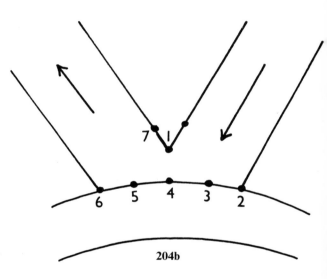

204b

Third method

(Refer to diagram 204c.) In this turning there is no completed edge to which the runners can be sewn and the lower edge 2–6 must be made at the same time as the turn. Work to 1 and make a back stitch at this hole. Work to 2 and make the edge stitch. Work through the coarse pair, tie the runners and work through two more pairs. ** Leave the runners and use the last pair they worked through as new runners to work to 3, where they make the edge stitch. Take the two bobbins inside the coarse thread, tie them three times and cut them off. Work back through three pairs and repeat from ** for holes 4 and 5 (do not take out a pair at 5). From 5 the runners work through to 1 to make up the back stitch there. Work to 6. Untwist the inner edge pair and weave the coarse thread between these two bobbins to lie as the thread next to the sewing

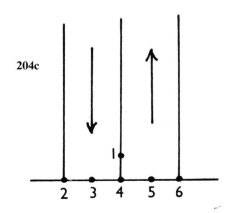

204c

edge. Continue the next section, after tying the runners at 6, and take sewings on the inner side.

These are general methods and must be adapted to suit each individual pattern. The number of pinholes along the base line may vary according to the width of the piece being turned and there may not be enough pairs to enable one to throw out a pair at the last hole or two of the turn. On the other hand, if there are too many pairs, making the clothwork too thick round the back stitch, one or two extra pairs may be taken out before the back stitch is made up.

Note 31   Starting at the head of a scroll

(Refer to diagrams 205a and 205b.) If the scroll is not too sharply turned, start towards the outer side of the head where a number of back stitches on the inner side will make it possible to get around without the use of any other method (diagram 205a).

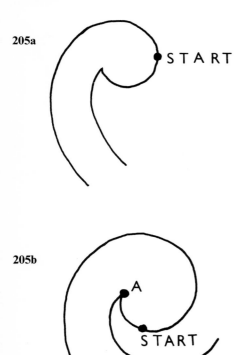

205a

START

205b

A

START

Remember to tie the runners *(note 5)* several times along the outside of the curve. If the scroll is sharply turned, proceed according to diagram 205b. Set up with eight pairs and a coarse pair, and work back and forth in the usual way, hanging in new pairs on the outside of the curve immediately; at hole A work a back stitch, which is not made up until the head of the scroll is turned. From A work to the outer side, make the edge stitch there and work back through three pairs only (i.e. the coarse pair and two more pairs). Leave the runners and take the last pair they worked through as new runners to the outer edge again where the next hole is worked. Bring the runners back through the coarse pair and leave them. Take the nearest of the downright pairs which were unworked in the previous row (the sixth pair counting from the outer side) in whole stitch to the outer edge.

* Make the next edge stitch, take the runners back through the coarse pair and leave them. Take the next of the unworked downright pairs in whole stitch to the outer edge and repeat from * until all the downright pairs except the inner coarse pair have been worked to the outer edge. If the head of the scroll is wide, it will be necessary to add several new pairs on the outer side while the turn is being made. Finally, the back stitch at A is made up, and the braid is continued normally. Several pairs will have to be taken out on the inside as the scroll narrows.

Note 32   Tiny leadworks in whole stitch ground

These spots are tiny leadworks which are made at random with the runners and the nearest unworked downright pair, using the leading runner bobbin as the weaver. When the leadwork is finished, continue the whole stitch with the weaver again used as one of the runners, but being very careful when working not to pull this thread tight so as to distort the leadwork. Keep the whole stitch fairly thin so that the spots will show up well.

Note 33a   Stamens for centre of flowers

(Refer to diagram 206a.) Set up at hole A with seven pairs. Work one hole of rib, and before making up the edge stitch at B, add one pair and lay it inside the first downright thread. Make up the edge stitch. Leave the outside edge pair and lift the next four pairs over it and use them to rib around the stamen. Tie the runners at the top hole of the stamen. After working hole C, take the runners back to the plain side, open out the first downright pair of the main rib, lift the four pairs which worked the rib of the stamen over the edge pair of the ring and lay them between these two bobbins. Tie twice over the bunch. Tie one pair from the bunch twice and cut out. Continue working the ribbed ring and repeat the process if other petals have stamens. When the rib has been joined at hole A, use the seven pairs to rib up and around the nearest petal.

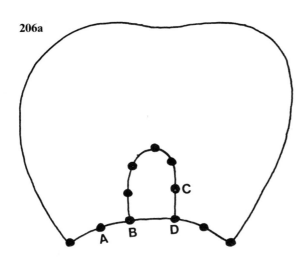

206a

Note 33b   Stamens which drop below the flower

(Refer to diagram 206b.) Set up five pairs at A. Rib to B, making the pinholes facing the flower. Rib to C, where one pair is hung in and laid aside. Rib to D. After setting the pin, work the runners through to the plain side, tie them twice, put all the other rib pairs between them and tie them

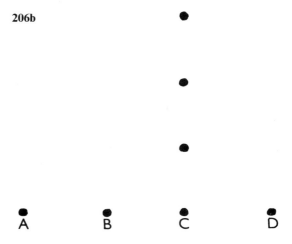

206b

twice over the bunch. Roll the tied pairs around the bunch once or twice to reach back to C, where all the bobbins are laid between the bobbins of the pair which was laid in and put aside here. This is now tied twice over them. Rib up to the flower and sew out.

Note 34a   Starting on a straight line of pinholes or working with pairs carried forward from another section

(Refer to diagram 207a.) Set up at No.1 with six pairs and a coarse pair. Work to hole 2 and add one pair *(note 2a)*. After making up the edge, work back through the coarse pair, tie the runners once, work one more pair, then * leave the runners and take the last pair they worked through as new runners to hole 3. Add one pair

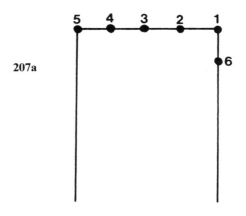

207a

here into the work and one pair to lay aside. Make up the edge. Work one pair and tie the runners *(note 5)*. Work one more pair. Repeat from * until hole 5 has been worked. (If there are more than five pinholes repeat from the *). After tying at pinhole 5, bring the pairs laid aside into position to fill the gaps where the turn has been made at each hole. Work across all the downrights in whole stitch. Set pin 6. Continue working the pattern.

Note 34b   Finishing on a straight line of pinholes

(Refer to diagram 207b.) Work to hole 1 and make a back stitch. Work to hole 2, make the edge stitch, work back through the coarse pair, tie the runners once to keep the point up against the pin and work through two more pairs. Leave the runners, and take the last pair they worked through as new runners to 3. Make the edge stitch. Take the first two bobbins inside the coarse thread, tie them three times and cut them off. * Work the runners through three pairs, leave them and use the last pair they passed through as new runners to work to 4. Make the edge stitch. Take the two bobbins inside the coarse thread, tie them three times and lay them back (do not cut them off). Repeat from * for hole 5, laying back another pair. Work across all downrights to 1, and make up the back stitch. Reduce to about six pairs; if necessary extra pairs may be taken out on the back stitch side of the work. Work to hole 6, add the pin and make up the edge, then cut out the coarse threads and take the runners through all remaining pairs, including the edge pair on the other side (without twisting). Tie all pairs three times, beginning with the runners. Bunch the bobbins, cross the outside pairs under the bunch and tie them three times over the bunch. Remove every alternate pin and push the remainder down into the pillow, leaving the last two or three on each side standing. The two pairs which were laid aside must now be spread out, so that one bobbin of each pair lies on each side of the lace. Turn all the bunched bobbins back over the lace between the standing pins and tie the spread pairs three times over the bunch. Cut off.

General Notes

Honiton lace is always made with the wrong side upwards. The fact that this lace has a wrong side limits its use, but it has the advantage that, having finished one part, the threads can be finished off neatly and taken across the lace already made to work the next part, without cutting the threads off.

Once the basic stitches have been mastered, the worker should watch the lace and not the bobbins, so as to be able to detect mistakes at once.

Always set pins in the pinholes slanting slightly outwards and backwards, otherwise the lace becomes longer than the pattern, the tension tends to become loose, and the lace will gradually rise from the pattern instead of remaining flat.

Pull the runners up well at the end of each row, work the first stitch through the coarse pair and again pull well – this will help to make small, neat pinholes.

Always keep the coarse threads close to the pins, and do not move the coarse bobbins unnecessarily across the pillow.

Do not lift the bobbins above the surface of the pillow.

Keep all threads and bobbins of similar length when working, about 8 to 10 cm (3 or 4 in.) of thread between bobbin and lace. The bobbins can then glide over each other and need no lifting.

Keep the pattern to be worked facing you, and

207b

move all the bobbins, except the coarse bobbins, well to obtain good tension.

Always twist bobbins right over left, hence, if one has to unpick to rectify mistakes, it is automatic to untwist left over right. The only exception to this rule is when making a left-hand purl *(note 9)*.

Do not wind too much thread onto the bobbins.

Study the pattern well before beginning the work: usually a flower, main stem or section must be worked first, so that other parts may be worked and attached to it. If you do not follow the correct order of working, you will have to put bobbins aside, until the main section has been worked.

When starting a ladder trail or twisted vein, twist the runners once in the first row, twice in the next row, and then continue with three twists. Reverse this process to close the vein – the start and finish will be much neater.

Remember, when working a purl edge, that fewer pairs will be needed, so take out one or two pairs according to the width of the section being worked.

Some pricking cards tend to be rather hard to prick; they can be softened and made more pliable if they are slightly warmed.

A good lacemaker should be able to use her patterns several times. Place a double piece of writing paper under the pattern after the first use. This will hold the pins firm where there are any worn or enlarged holes. On the other hand, it is false economy to use any pattern too often, as small particles of card can get worked into the lace and are difficult to remove.

Always cover the pillow with a cover cloth when it is not in use.

Do not handle threads more than necessary. The needlepin should be used to lengthen or shorten threads. To shorten threads, insert the point of the needlepin into the loop of the hitch on the bobbin. Pull the loop away from the bobbin and wind the bobbin towards you, easing the loop with the needlepin as you wind. When lengthening the bobbin, the thread sometimes becomes caught behind other threads and can be loosened with the needlepin in the same way.

When starting a leaf, an experienced worker will tie the runners after passing through the coarse pair, after each of the first two pins have been set. This results in neater pinholes at the top. This also applies when starting a braid for which pairs have been sewn or laid in.

Always keep lace and thread in blue paper, and away from daylight, to keep it white and clean.

10
Mounting Honiton Lace on Material

There are several methods of mounting lace on material, the most common are the following:

Method 1   Lace stitch
(three-sided punch stitch)

(Refer to photograph 208 and diagram 209.) First, tack the material to a strip of sugar paper, then tack the lace on to the material so that the pinholes lie correctly on the weave of the material; make the tacking stitches so that they do not interfere with the pinholes on the edge of the lace where the punch stitches will be worked.

Extreme care must be taken when tacking the lace to the material if a satisfactory result is to be achieved. For the punch stitch I recommend using a size 6 sewing needle and the thread used for making the lace; if this is very fine a slightly stronger lace cotton can be used, as a certain amount of strength is required while working.

Working from right to left, * bring the needle out at A in the material, insert it at B (the distance between A and B will be determined by the distance between the pinholes of the lace), bring it out at A, insert again at B and bring it out again at A. This makes two back stitches over

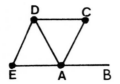

209

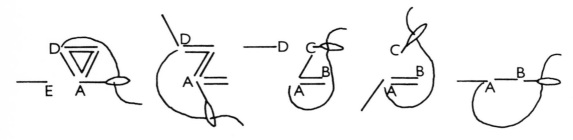

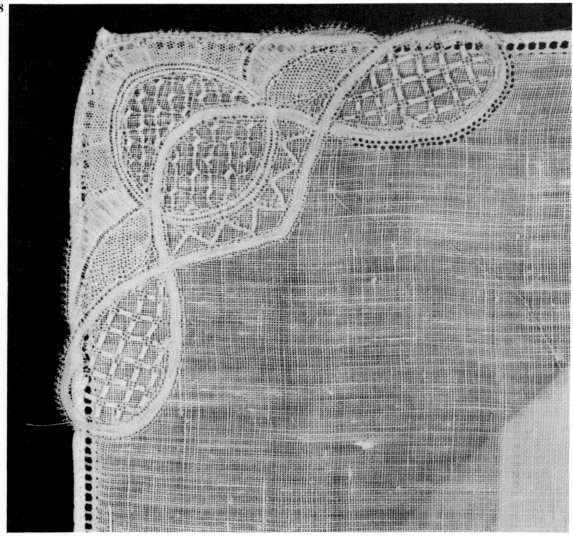

each other. Next insert the needle at C through a pinhole of the lace and the material at the back, bring it out at A, insert it at C and bring it out at D. (The needle brought out at D comes through the material at the back and through a pinhole of the lace.) Two stitches are then made in the same way between C and D; after finally emerging at D, the needle is inserted at A, brought out at D, inserted at A and brought out at D. Repeat from *, continuing in this manner until the sewing is completed. Turn the work over, remove the paper and cut away the material close to the stitching.

Method 2   Rolled and whipped

(Refer to photograph 210.) Tack the material to a piece of sugar paper and the lace to the material as described in the first method. Use a size 12 needle and the thread used to make the lace. Hem the lace to the material with small stitches using each pinhole, making a double stitch occasionally. When complete, remove the paper, cut away the material at the back an inch at a time, leaving about $\frac{1}{8}$ in. to be rolled and whipped with small firm stitches; roll the edge away from the lace, pushing the raw edge under with the

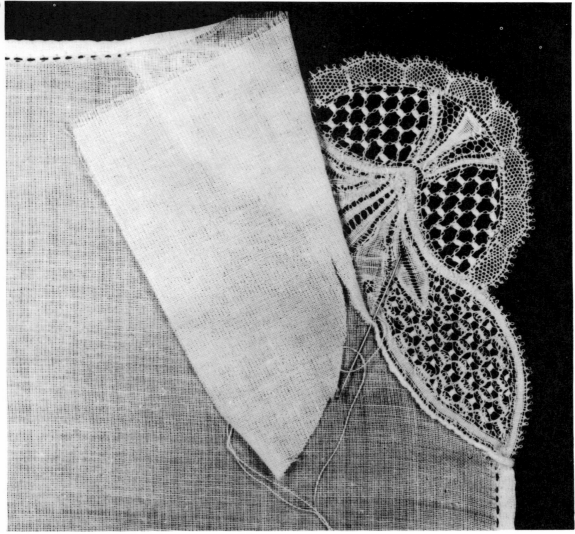

point of the needle. Insert the needle under the roll, bring it out at the top of the roll but not into the actual lace edge. Continue to cut small lengths of the material, roll and whip.

Method 3   Picot edging

(Refer to photograph 211 and diagrams 212a and 212b.) A method of attaching a corner motif which leaves most of the surrounding edge in need of finishing. This is based on a form of four-sided stitch.

Cut a piece of fabric $\frac{1}{2}$ in. larger all around, cut along the line of a drawn thread. Draw one thread $\frac{1}{2}$ in. within the outer edge, which outlines actual size. Position the motif so that each end of the long side registers with the line of the drawn out thread marking the actual size, making sure it is set square and tack.

Use the same thread as used in the lace and a No. 6 sharps or betweens needle. The size of the block is determined by the spacing of the pin-holes, not always following the grain or straight of fabric. Begin by attaching the motif to the

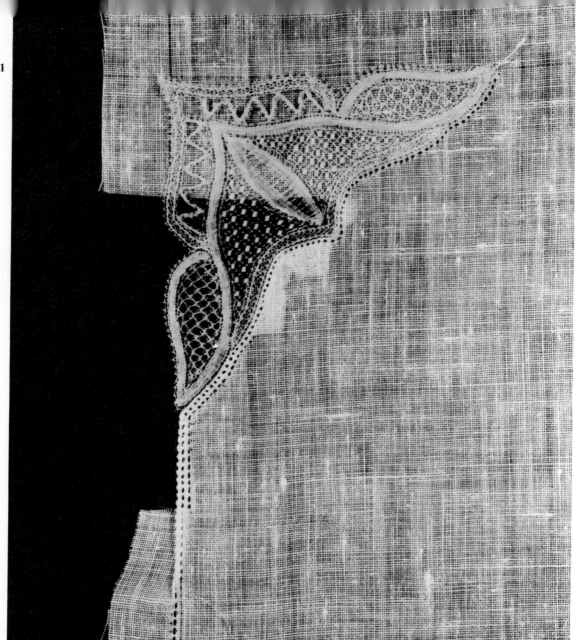

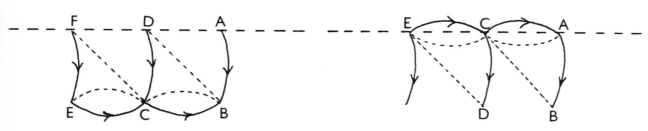

212a

212b

fabric so as to become accustomed to the size of block. Follow diagram 212a: bring needle out at A through linen and pinhole when attaching motif, insert needle at B – out at C, insert needle at B – out at D, insert needle at C – out at E, insert needle at C – out at F and so on. At the end of the motif continue along next side following diagram 212b: bring needle out at A, insert at B – out at C, insert needle at A – out at C, insert needle at D – out at E; pull stitch as tight as thread will allow. Make the same size block as needed when attaching the motif. Complete circumference of handkerchief.

Turn fabric to under side commencing at the line of the drawn out thread and pinhole edge. Fabric will need to be slashed to make a close turn on an undulating curve. The second row is worked over the top of the first row. Follow diagram 212a and work a full circuit over double fabric. At this stage a picot edge appears on unattached edges. Cut away surplus fabric from under side, close to stitches.

To enclose all signs of raw edges another circuit following diagram 212a can be worked to form a second row of blocks immediately innermost of the first row. The result justly rewards the effort.

Method 4   To mount edgings onto net (for wedding veils, etc.)

(Refer to diagram 213.) Having made quite sure that your net has been evenly cut, tack it to strips of sugar paper, allowing the paper to be twice the width of the lace. Tack the lace on to the net, leaving about 1 in. of net outside the edge of the lace, A. With a number 12 sewing needle and the thread used for the lace, oversew into each hole of the inner braid of the lace edging, making a back stitch occasionally, B. When complete, remove the paper and cut away the surplus net, leaving about $\frac{1}{4}$ in., C; the raw edge will not be visible on the right side. Motifs can be mounted inside the border in a similar way, tack the net to a piece of paper and then the motif to the net. Sew to the net but do not cut away at the back.

Notes on washing lace

Much lace which has become discoloured and soiled can be washed and the appearance greatly improved. All lace, especially very soiled and delicate old lace, will need as little handling as possible. Silk lace does not wash or clean well. The best way to treat most other types is to soak well and long in cold water; this removes a surprising amount of dirt. Use pure soap flakes, well dissolved in an enamelled saucepan; add the lace and boil gently for one minute. Discard the soapy water, repeating this process until no further dirt can be removed. Rinse well in cold water, roll in a clean cloth and press out as much water as possible. When still slightly damp, pin into shape and press carefully, using a cool iron, with the right side of the lace downwards. Brown stains often found on old lace will not be removed by boiling, but can be gently dabbed with salts of lemon or thymol crystals which may be obtained from a good chemist. For larger pieces of lace, enclose in a pillow case and wash gently in warm water with pure soap flakes. Always store lace in acid-free tissue.

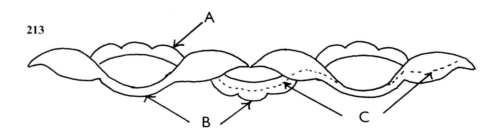

213

Grid Prickings

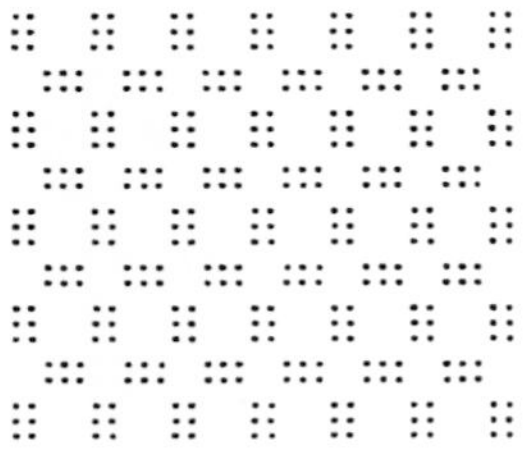

1   Snatch Bar and Leadworks

2   Toad in the Hole Variation

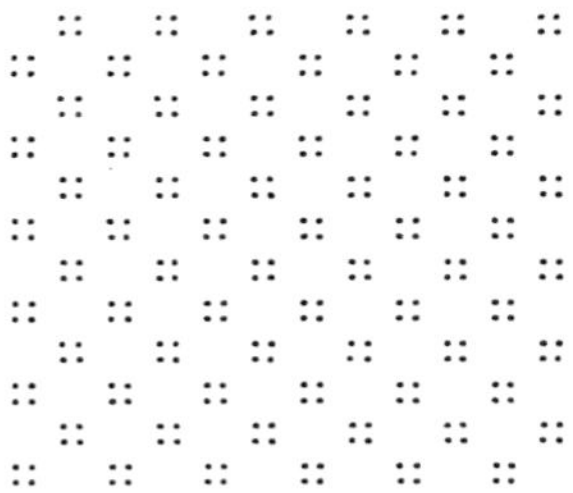

3   Diamond

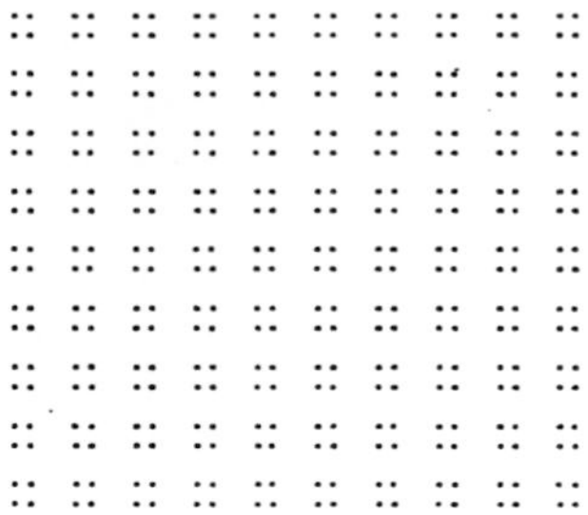

4   Blossom

5   Whole Stitch Block Variation

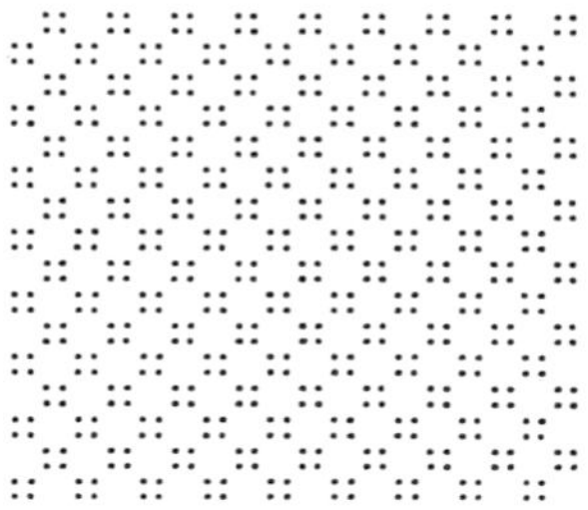

6   Four Pin

138

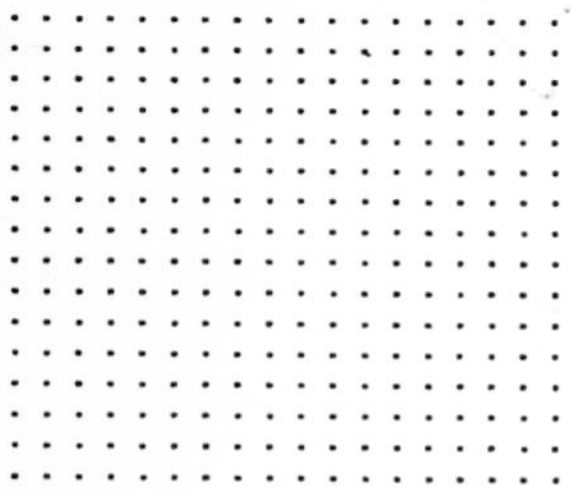

7 Brick

8 Pin and a Stitch and Net

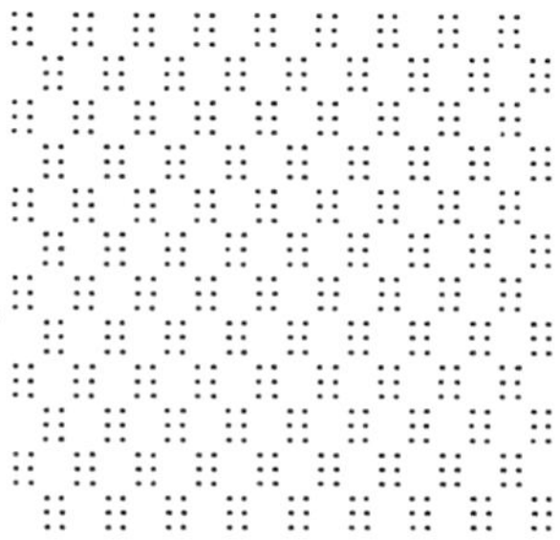

9 Toad in the Hole

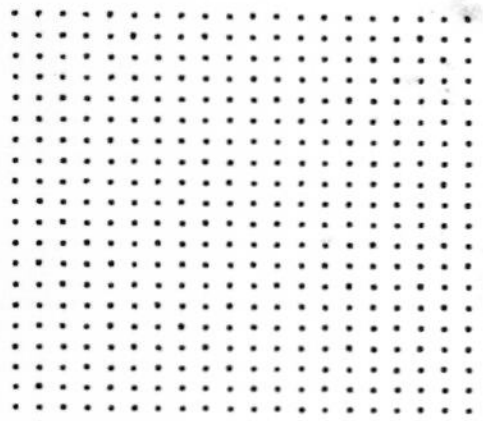

10 Pin and a Chain

11 Straight Pin

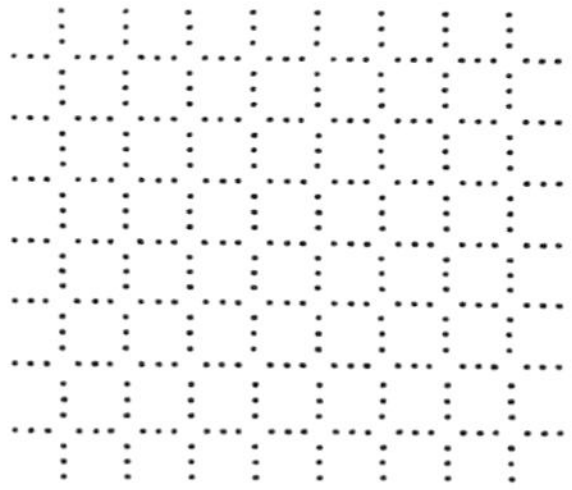

12 Rib squares and Leadwork

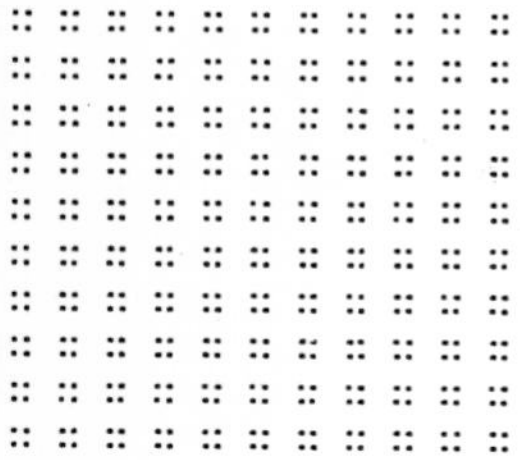

13 Jubilee

14 Four Pin and Leadwork

Bibliography

Treadwin, *Antique Point and Honiton Lace*, (Ward Lock & Tyler, London, first published 1874)

Devonia, *The Honiton Lace Book*, (The Bazaar Office, London, first published 1873; reprinted by Paul Minet, London, 1972)

Maidment, Margaret, *A Manual of Hand-Made Bobbin Lace*, (Charles T Branford Co, Boston, 1954; reprinted by Piccadilly Rare Books, Paul Minet, London)

Palliser, *The History of Lace*, (E. P. Publishing Ltd, first published 1902)

Penderel Moody, A., *Devon Pillow Lace*, (Cassell & Co Ltd, first published 1907)

List of Suppliers

UK

E Braggins & Sons
26–36 Silver Street
Bedford
Bedfordshire

Mace & Nairn
89 Crane Street
Salisbury SP1 2PY
Wiltshire

A Sells
Lane Cove
49 Pedley Lane
Clifton, Shefford, Beds

D J Hornsby
149 High Street
Burton Latimer
Kettering, Northants

Ye Honiton Lace Shoppe
44 High Street
Honiton
Devon

Christopher Williams
23 St Leonards Road
Bournemouth
Dorset BH8 8QL
(old and new lace books)

USA

Baltazor, Inc.
3262 Severn Avenue
Metairie, LA 7002

Berga-Ullman, Inc.
P.O. Box 918
North Adams, MA 01247

Frederick J. Fawcett
129 South Street
Boston, MA 02130

Happy Hands
3007 S. W. Marshall
Pendleton, OR 97108

Lace Place de Belgique
800 S.W. 17th Street
Boca Raton, FL 33432

Lacis
Antique Lace & Textiles
2150 Stuart Street
Berkeley, CA 97705

Robin & Russ Handweavers
533 N. Adam Street
McMinnville, OR 97128

Robin's Bobbins
Rte. 1 — Box 294A
Mineral Bluff, GA 30559

Osma G. Tod Studio
319 Mendoza Avenue
Coral Gables, FL 33134

Van Sciver Bobbin Lace Supply
310 Aurora Street
Ithaca, N.Y. 14850

The Unique and Art Lace Cleaners
5926 Delmar Boulevard
St. Louis, MO 63112

The World in Stitches
82 South Street
Milford, N.H. 03055

Or your local bookseller

Index